Educating the Heart
Lessons to Build
Respect and Responsibility

Frank Siccone
Siccone Institute, San Francisco

Lilia López
Alexandria City Public Schools

Allyn and Bacon
Boston London Toronto Sydney Tokyo Singapore

Copyright © 2000 by Allyn & Bacon
A Pearson Education Company
160 Gould Street
Needham Heights, Massachusetts 02494-2130

Internet: www.abacon.com

ISBN 0-205-31364-7

Printed in the United States of America

10 9 8 7 6 5 4 3 2 1   03 02 01 00 99

DEDICATION

From Frank Siccone

I was fortunate enough to have two fathers, and I dedicate this book to them:

- My biological dad — the original Frank Siccone — who gave me my life and my Italian heritage which I treasure. He always accepted me for who I am, and treated me as someone special. I also appreciate that he chose for my mother the woman with the biggest heart.

- My stepfather — Joe Samson — who loved my mother and supported her devotion to her sons, her grandchildren and great grandchildren. He contributed to all of us in many ways throughout the years.

From Lilia López

This book is dedicated to my greatest treasures on this planet:

- My mother — Marie La Bar, whose constant faith and pride in me have inspired me all of my life.

- My children — Lisa, Michael, Tomás, and Alejhandro López whose presence in the world have brought me great joy and pride.

- My grandchildren — Michael, Veronica, Gabriela, and Jonathan Paul, whose future depends on what we do today. May they live in a world where they are celebrated and loved by just being who they are.

CONTENTS

INTRODUCTION

Educating the mind without educating the heart is no education at all.

—Aristotle

What's Going On?

School-related incidences of intolerance — slurs, taunts, graffiti, intimidation and violence stemming from prejudice because of race, ethnicity, religion, gender, sexual orientation or disability — appear to be on the rise. In fact, it is estimated that more than ten percent of the hate crimes reported to the FBI by U.S. police departments in 1997 occurred at schools.[1] In California alone, 21,438 violent crimes were reported in the state's public schools in 1998.[2]

Media accounts include:

- White high school students in Rhode Island waving a Confederate flag and chanting racial slurs at Hispanic players on a visiting basketball team.

- An accomplished African American basketball player in Sacramento, California became the target of death threats by vandals who painted "KKK" and swastikas on school buildings.

- Hispanic and black students at a high school in Los Angeles engaged in a bottle-throwing race war that had to be broken up by police in riot gear.

- In Marin County — just north of San Francisco — a 17-year-old gay student was beaten unconscious, and the word "fag" had been carved into his arm and stomach by his assailants.

Parents who believe their children have a right to attend schools free from harassment and harm are filing lawsuits against school officials who fail to create an atmosphere that is safe, secure and peaceful.

One such case in Tempe, Arizona involved a 14-year-old student who was repeatedly called "nigger" by other students. The judge upholding the parent's case said, "It does not take an educational psychologist to conclude that being referred to by one's peers by the most noxious racial epithet in the contemporary American lexicon, being shamed and humiliated on the basis of one's race, and having the school authorities ignore or reject one's complaint would adversely affect a black child's ability to obtain the same benefit from schooling as her white counterparts."

In response to the escalating number of incidents, the U.S. Department of Education sent a guidebook on "Protecting Students from Harassment and Hate Crimes" to every school district in the nation. Some educators would argue that they are being asked to fix a problem that goes far beyond what is taught in schools. Certainly, schools are a microcosm of society at large, and they can not single-handedly eliminate racism, gender inequalities and homophobia. Schools do, however, have an important role to play, and a significant contribution to make.

Toward a Culture of Respect

The purpose of this book is to give educators — teachers, administrators, counselors, instructional aides, resource staff, parents, and so forth — tools that they can use to teach students to respect themselves and others.

Students who attend classes that are geared only to the "mainstream" culture — where no recognition is given to the legitimacy of other cultures — are likely to feel isolated and inferior. It should be no surprise that the students who tend to have the most difficulty in school (Native Americans, African Americans and Hispanics) are from groups who have experienced a long history of subjugation, prejudice and discrimination.[3] What happens to a child when — as Adrienne Rich expresses it — "someone with the authority of a teacher" presents a portrait of America, and "you are not in it" . . . "a moment of psychic disequilibrium, as if you looked into a mirror and saw nothing."[4]

We need to consider the role that schools and society in general have in creating low self-esteem in children. That is, students do not simply develop poor self-concepts out of the blue. Rather they are the result of policies and practices of schools and society that respect and affirm some groups while devaluing and rejecting others.

— Sonia Nieto

In order for children to develop a healthy sense of self, they need to experience themselves as unique individuals who are accepted for who they are. They need to feel that they belong, that they are important members of their families, their circle of friends and their communities. They also need to know that they are capable of achieving their goals and realizing their dreams. This can only really occur in a bias-free environment that sincerely values all people equally.

Self-esteem — "the disposition to experience oneself as competent to cope with the challenges of life and as deserving of happiness"[5] — involves an interactive relationship between oneself and one's environment. What we believe about ourselves determines how we relate to others. Their feedback, in turn, affects how we feel about ourselves, and so forth.

Educating the Heart is structured into four parts as shown in the following chart:

	Experience (Internal)	Express (External)
Others	Interdependence 2.	Social Responsibility 4.
Self	Independence 1.	Personal Responsibility 3.

Specifically, Part I of the book is focused on the internal experience of self-respect that includes a recognition of oneself as an independent, autonomous being who is unique in all the world. Issues of *identity* are dealt with such as: Who am I? What makes me me? How am I the same and how am I different from others? What makes me special?

Part II is involved with the experience of our interdependence. In order for our schools, our communities, our society, our world to be truly functional, everyone must be valued. This section is related to the need to *belong*, connectedness, affiliation and friendship.

Part III is related to personal responsibility which is a logical expression of self-esteem. This section is designed to help students increase their sense of *power* to control their lives and expand their ability to be successful. Achievement, purposefulness, self-directedness, risk taking and goal attainment are all part of this.

Part IV, *social responsibility,* is intended to encourage students to move beyond personal self-interest to accepting greater responsibility for the world around them. Activities are included to develop students' social and interpersonal skills which are becoming increasingly important as more and more schools use cooperative learning methods, and a growing number of businesses are using work teams to improve productivity. The second half of this final section is devoted to the significant role that *contribution* and service play in people's experience of happiness and self-worth. We believe that every human being has as his/her purpose the desire to make a difference—a positive difference expressed in some unique way.

Children who accept themselves as worthwhile are more likely to accept and value others. Children who have confidence in themselves are more apt to participate actively, take greater risks and find new ways to overcome obstacles to their success. Children who feel included as valued members of society are less likely to vandalize it. Children who feel capable of living meaningful lives are less likely to waste theirs.

> *No one has yet fully realized the wealth of sympathy, kindness and generosity hidden in the soul of a child. The effort of every true education should be to unlock that treasure.*
>
> — Emma Goldman

Now for the Most Important Variable — YOU

> *Modeling is not the best way to teach. It is the only way to teach.*
>
> — Albert Schweitzer

Research indicates that students pick up on teachers' attitudes even when the teacher is unaware of having negative feelings.

You can't teach what you don't know, and you can't give what you don't have.

Your own feelings of self-worth, and self-efficacy are essential to your ability to support your students in building their self-respect. Likewise your attitudes toward accepting and encouraging all students are critical to your creating a safe and supportive classroom environment. In essence, you must become both a self-actualized and a multicultural person[6] which involves an appreciation for learning as a life-long process, an openness to viewing things from various perspectives, a willingness to confront your own prejudices, and a commitment to esteeming yourself and others — all others.

It is strongly recommended that you do all the activities in this book yourself before using them with your students so that you experience them as a participant and have the opportunity to process through any issues that arise for yourself. When conducting the activities with students, it is important that you take an active role — demonstrating an appropriate level of self-disclosure, risk-taking and enthusiasm for the process.

The activities are not intended to be done in isolation but rather, they are meant to serve as catalysts for creating an inclusive and esteeming environment that is ongoing. Respect for self and others does not end when the activity is over. You are welcome to do the activities in sequence or pick and choose the ones that are most appropriate for you and your students. Not all the activities are suitable for all grade levels. Those requiring a lot of writing or the analysis of complex feelings would need to be simplified when being used with younger children. Some of the activities can be done in a few minutes at the beginning or end of the day, or when you want to change the energy level in the classroom. Many of the exercises will take the equivalent of a full class period and a few could be extended over a period of days or weeks.

As much as possible, integrate the material into your regular routine. "Promises to Keep" (Activity 27), "My Circle of Friends" (Activity 28), and "Let There Be Peace on Earth: Conflict Management" (Activity 68) could be used as part of your classroom management program. "SHARE to Show You Care" (Activity 52), "Are You Listening?" (Activity 53) and "Team Problem Solving" (Activity 56) could be used in conjunction with cooperative learning. A number of the lessons could serve as the focus of a theme-based unit of study to which all academic subjects could be related. "The Joy of Eating" (Activity 19), "The Cultures We Are" (Activity 21), and "Community-Service Projects" (Activity 73) are some examples.

Children learn not just by what they are told, but also by what they see and feel for themselves. The more aspects of the school environment that are involved, the more successful any program will be. Respect for self and others needs to be practiced not only in the formalized curriculum but also in the "covert curriculum." The values, attitudes, beliefs and actions of staff and students, school policies and politics, teaching and learning styles, assessment procedures and community involvement all teach very clear lessons. Perhaps you could enlist the support of your colleagues in adapting the activities in this book into a school-wide program.

Our purpose for writing this book is to contribute to you, and we are certain that your purpose in reading it is to contribute to your students. We trust that, in turn, your students will be inspired by a new vision of what is possible for them: a vision where everyone is included, everyone is valued, everyone is successful and everyone contributes. The possibilities are limitless!

The very intention to teach is an act of love.

— Frank Siccone

Notes

1. Erin McCormick, "Schools Feel Heat of Hate" *San Francisco Chronicle* (February 21, 1999), p A-1.

2. Thomas A. Ruppanner, "We Must Bring an End to School Violence" *San Francisco Chronicle* (March 24, 1999), p A-19.

3. Jim Cummins, *Empowering Minority Students.* (Sacramento, CA: California Association of Bilingual Education, 1989), p 8.

4. Adrienne Rich, *Blood, Bread and Poetry: Selective Prose, 1979-1985.* (New York: Norton, 1986), p 199.

5. Nathaniel Brandon, *The Power of Self-Esteem.* (Deerfield Beach, FL: Health Communications, Inc., 1992), pp 17-20.

6. Sonia Nieto, *Affirming Diversity: The Sociopolitical Context of Multicultural Education.* (White Plains, NY: Longman, 1992), p 275.

ACKNOWLEDGMENTS

From Frank Siccone

I am truly blessed and deeply grateful to the many people who have contributed to my happiness and success.

For support with this book I am indebted to the following people:

- Robert Wright for doing an outstanding job with research assistance, manuscript preparation, and a zillion other things — all done with a spirit of love, caring and commitment to quality.

- My educator friends including: Esther Wright, Hanoch McCarty, Joe Fimiani, and Jack Canfield — all of whom have contributed significantly to my work over the years.

- Norris Harrell, my new editor at Allyn and Bacon for helping get this book published in record time.

- Chris Jehle, my incredibly supportive partner, for editing and proofreading this and all my other books as well.

From Lilia López

I have been blessed beyond my wildest imagination with unconditional love and support in my life.

Some that have supported me and shared many universal truths with me include:

- Cheryl Chang, a loving and enthusiastic classroom teacher, who taught me how to create win-win situations that changed my life forever.

- Jane C. Wilhite, Bruce Conching, Brian Klemmer, Lance Giroux, and Dan Dorr for teaching me how to create balance, peace, and success in my life.

- Frank Siccone, who saw the potential for me to make a contribution to his life's work.

PART I

SELF–RESPECT AND INDEPENDENCE

Freedom to Be Me

Of every hue and caste am I,
I resist any thing better than my own diversity.

— Walt Whitman

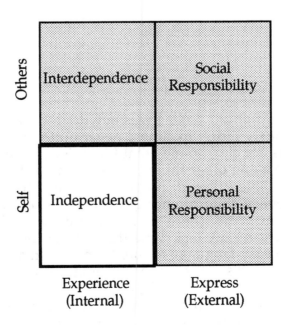

CHAPTER ONE

Identity

Who Am I?

Be humble, for the worst thing in the world is of the same stuff as you; be confident, for the stars are of the same stuff as you.

—Nicholai Velimirovic

Introduction

As a seven year old child I was bewildered to find myself with a teacher who obviously didn't like me. I never quite understood what the problem was. It was not clear to me what I had done wrong or what was the matter with me. Among other things, my second grade teacher insisted on calling me Francis, even though no one else ever used that name. Her rationale was that every child attending Catholic school had to have been named after a saint, and there is no "Saint Frank." She also persisted in mispronouncing my last name throughout the school year. Maybe Italian was not an easy language for her to master In any case, I felt devalued and diminished, and spent the year wishing I could just disappear.

Needless to say, a student in hiding, trying to be invisible, is not likely to be a very active participant in the learning process. A child's name is an important part of his/her identity, and should be treated with respect.

The activities in this first chapter revolve around using names to build connections and instill a feeling of pride. They are meant to bolster your students' sense of independence, making it safe for them to be themselves in all their uniqueness and express themselves in all their wonderfulness.

1

The Name Game

> *I am the one whose love overcomes you, already with you when you think to call my name.*
>
> —Jane Kenyon

*Background**

This first section of the book deals with one of the fundamental building blocks of self-esteem — a sense of identity. The experience of valuing myself is predicated on the awareness of myself as a distinct, unique individual.

Virtually all cultures provide for the need for self-identity by using names to distinguish one person from another, although the approach to naming may differ.

- Many children are named after a close relative or friend of the family. Sharing a name with someone can create a special bond.

- The day of birth is commonly used in Tibet as the source of a baby's name: Sunday, *Nyma*; Monday, *Dawa*; Tuesday, *Mingma*.

- Names based upon things in nature are used by the Miwok Indians of California: "Iskemu," water running gently when the creek dries; "Kono," a squirrel biting through the center of a pine nut.

- In Hawaii, an event that occurred at the time of birth often serves as the inspiration for a name. "Kapaulehuaonapalilahilahiokaala"

---

* The background information regarding naming customs from diverse cultures was found in *Mamatoto: A Celebration of Birth* by Carroll Dunham and The Body Shop Team, New York: Penguin Books, 1991.

means the lehua flower blooming on the step of ridges of Mount Kaula.

- People who believe in reincarnation seek to discover the child's true name. The Dyak of Borneo, for example, offer the baby a bundle of reeds with the names of ancestors inscribed on them. The one that the child touches is assumed to be the correct name.

Purpose

Since one significant aspect of our identity is our name, exploring the origins and significance of your students' names with them can help strengthen their sense of being unique.

This series of exercises will also increase students' appreciation for their own and other cultures, given that most names have associations with one's family, ethnic group, religion, and so forth.

The first activity is a good "ice breaker" on the first day of school in that it helps students remember each other's name in a way that is fun and exciting.

Procedure

1. Have students sit in a circle, or divide them into two or three circles of ten or so.

2. Introduce the activity as being a fun and easy way of learning each other's names.

3. Explain that each student will introduce him or herself by first name and a word that describes how he/she is feeling this morning. The word is to begin with the same first letter or sound as the student's name to give an association that will help the others in remembering the student's name.

   Give examples such as:

   "Hi, I'm **D**orothy and I'm **d**elighted to be here."

   "Hi, I'm **K**ris and I feel **c**ool."

   "Hi, I'm **A**lonzo and I'm **a**lert."

4. Start the process yourself or ask for a volunteer to begin. Going clockwise around the circle, the second person first states the name and adjective of the person to his or her right and then states his or her own name and descriptive word.

The third person repeats what the first and second students have said and so forth around the circle until the last person begins with the first person and continues around the circle remembering each of the students names and adjectives.

5. Students often get excited and tend to help out if the person whose turn it is has trouble remembering. We suggest that the student who is speaking be given a chance to do it on his or her own. If help is needed, he or she can request it.

6. At the end of the activity, allow the students to share their feelings about doing the exercise. You may also want to read them a book about names, *Adelaide to Zeke* by Janet Wolf (New York: Harper & Row, 1977).

Other books — selected for their thematic relevance to the activities — are listed in the back of each chapter. This section includes a number of stories of children whose names are clearly culture specific. You may want to read one of these in conjunction with each of the activities in this chapter.

When reading books to your students, it is always helpful to hold the book up to show the pictures. Another way to have everyone see the pictures is to duplicate each page of the book onto an overhead transparency and show that transparency as you read that page in the book. It will help hold the students' attention.

2

The Name Game — II

Purpose

This is essentially the same as Activity 1 with a slight variation. This works well on the second day to reinforce students' memories of each other's names.

It is also an opportunity for students to affirm a positive attribute or strength that they possess.

Procedure

1.   Set up the exercise with students in a circle, the same as Activity 1.

2.   This time when the students introduce themselves, they are to state a positive attribute, strength, talent or skill that they have. A list of positive feeling words is provided for your reference. Once again, they are to use an adjective that starts with the same first letter or sound of their name.

   Give them examples such as:

   "Hi, I'm **D**imitri and I **d**ance well."

   "Good morning, I'm **H**anoch and I'm **h**onest."

   "I'm **E**ssence and I'm **e**nergetic."

   "I'm **A**lejandro and I'm **a**wesome."

POSITIVE FEELING WORDS (Partial List)

adorable

adoring

beautiful

blissful

calm

celebrating

centered

cheerful

confident

content

delighted

ecstatic

elegant

enchanted

energetic

enjoying

enthusiastic

excellent

excited

exhilarated

fun-loving

fulfilled

gentle

glad

gorgeous

grateful

gratified

great

handsome

happy

hilarious

honest

intelligent

jolly

joyous

jubilant

kind

lively

lovely

loving

merry

mirthful

neat

nice

outrageous

overjoyed

peaceful

pleasant

pleased

quick

quiet

rapturous

ravishing

rejoicing

relaxed

relishing

reveling

satisfied

serene

soaring

stunning

tender

thrilled

tranquil

triumphant

understanding

vivacious

wonderful

yummy

zany

Suggestion: Let the students brainstorm their own list of adjectives. They will come up with some amazing words. (Slang words should be accepted. If inappropriate language is suggested, you could use this as an opportunity to discuss what makes some words offensive, and ask the students to agree only to use words that are acceptable to everyone in the class.)

3

Name Toss

> **A** *man who finds no satisfaction in himself, seeks for it in vain elsewhere.*
>
> —La Rochefoncauld

Purpose

This activity builds on the previous ones, and can be used, once again, to help students remember the names of their classmates. It is also an opportunity for the students to give and receive positive feedback from one another.

Materials

One of the following for each group of students:

Basketball
Soccer ball
Tennis ball
Frisbee
Koosh ball (available in rainbow colors)
Heart shaped bean bag

Procedure

1. This activity can be done outdoors as a PE exercise with the students standing in a circle using a basketball, soccer ball, pine cone, tennis ball, or frisbee. The smaller objects, koosh ball or bean bag, can be used if the activity is done in the classroom with the students seated in a circle. You can divide the class into groups of around ten students per group or keep the entire class together.

2. Describe the activity and then begin it yourself or ask for a volunteer.

3.   The first person calls out the name of someone else in the circle and says something positive about him or her — something he or she likes or admires about this other student — while tossing the ball or object.

4.   The student who receives the object, in turn, calls out the name and positive attribute of another while tossing the object to this next person.

5.   The activity continues until everyone has been called. Each student can be called only once.

Only positive statements are allowed.

Name Flag

> **A** man's name is not like a mantle which merely hangs about him, and which one perchance may safely twitch and pull, but a perfectly fitting garment, which, like the skin, has grown over him, at which one cannot rake and scrape without injuring the man himself.
>
> —Goethe

Purpose

This is an art activity that will allow students to increase their sense of identity while linking their name with their country of origin.

Materials

One piece of art paper for each student
Crayons, colored marking pens or paints

Procedure

1. Prior to the day of the activity, have students research the colors of the flag of their country of origin.

    Encourage them to trace their ancestry back to another country and find a picture of the country's flag to discover what colors are used.

    In cases where students' families have immigrated from more than one country, students could pick the one with which they most identify, or the one that is least common, or the one they like the best.

    If some students don't know what colors to use or don't want to use the colors of their country's flag, they could choose colors that are important to them.

2.   Hand out the art supplies and ask the students to write or print their name on the page as large as possible.

3.   Next have them draw random lines over the page to create an abstract design.

4.   Now instruct them to color in each space using one of the colors of their country's flag. Each adjoining space should be a different color.

5.   Let students hang their flags on a bulletin board in the classroom or in one of the school's corridors.

Ask the students to explain their designs, the colors used, what makes them unique, and so forth.

6.   Discuss with your students what they learned from doing the activity. Encourage students to discover the symbolism of the colors and designs used in their country's flags.

5

*Let Your Fingers Do the Talking**

> *T*he highest result of education is tolerance.
>
> —Helen Keller

Purpose

By learning their name in another language—Braille—students will have another opportunity to strengthen their sense of identity while learning something about their visually - handicapped peers.

Procedure

1.   Begin by asking your students a series of questions such as:

   How many of you know someone who is blind or visually handicapped?

   Do you know how people who are not sighted read and write?

   How many of you know what Braille is?

   Where have you seen Braille used? (Some elevators and ATM machines have Braille instructions posted.)

---

* Reprinted from *Children of the Rainbow- First Grade* by permission of the Board of Education of the City of New York. This New York City Board of Education Rainbow resource guide for teachers/curricula is not affiliated with the original Children of the Rainbow by Fern S. Keiner (a/k/a Rainbow Children) (i) trade name (a licensed business since 1970) and (ii) early childhood beginning reading program and brotherhood publications and music copyrighted 1969, 1970 by Fern S. Keiner (music publisher with ASCAP) and should not be confused with her business or publications.

2.   Let your students know that today they are going to learn how to write their names in Braille. Hand out copies of the Braille Alphabet Worksheet and My Name in Braille Worksheet.

3.   Ask students to take the My Name in Braille Worksheet and print their first name in the top row of boxes; one letter in each box.

4.   *Next, look up each letter in the Braille alphabet and color in the appropriate dots in the box below each letter of your first name. Fill in each box until you have spelled out the letters in your name.*

5.   Have the students hold up their completed My Name in Braille Worksheet to share with their classmates.

Variation I

Since Braille is meant to be read with fingers, not eyes, you may want to give students a way of making their name in Braille tactile by having them glue split peas onto the circles that they colored in with pencil.

Variation II

The same activity could be done using any language. Those based upon a writing system different from the English alphabet — Hebrew, Japanese, and so forth — would be particularly interesting.

You could also teach your students how to use American Sign Language (ASL) to spell out their names.

Braille Alphabet Worksheet

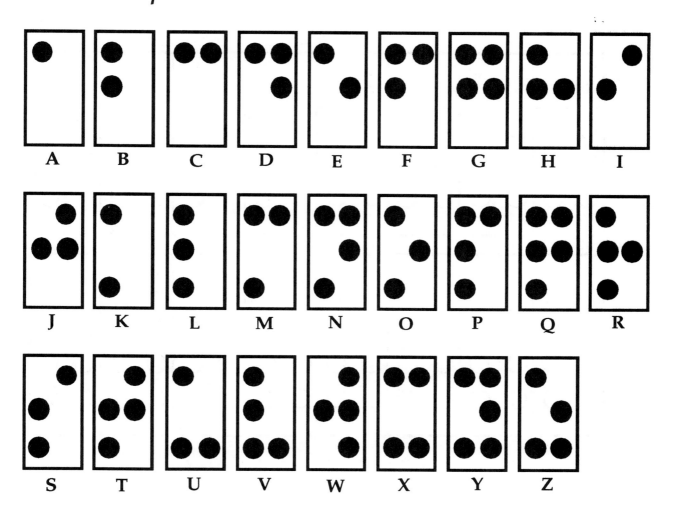

My Name in Braille Worksheet

Name Interviews

> **S**ay
> *who I am.*
> *Set*
> *our two fires climbing.*
>
> —Mary Virginia Micka

Purpose

For students to deepen their sense of identity by discussing the significance of their names, including their thoughts and feelings, family association, cultural connections, and so forth.

Procedure

1. Have students find a partner. There are a number of creative ways of doing this including:

   Find someone who is wearing the same color shoes as you are.

   Line up according to birthday and pair up with the person whose birthday is closest to yours.

   Find someone whose Name Flag has the same colors as yours.

   Count the number of letters in your first name. If you have an even number of letters find a partner whose name also has an even number. If your name has an odd number of letters find a partner whose name has an odd number.

2. Instruct the students to take turns interviewing each other about their names. Whenever students are working in pairs, encourage

them to sit facing each other to enhance their communication and sense of connection.

You may hand out a copy of the Name Interview Worksheet to each pair of students or put the questions on the board.

Note: *In addition to or instead of the questions on the worksheet, you can let the students ask any other questions that they have about their partner's name. A good rule here is that students can ask any question they want, provided it is a question they would be willing to answer themselves. Also, students should always be given the option to pass.*

3.   Bring the students together to discuss what they learned about each other and about how people get named. You can structure this by having students introduce their partner, telling the class some fun facts about their partner's name.

Continue the discussion by focusing on cultural aspects of your students' names, for example,

- The common practice in Spanish-speaking nations to use both the father's surname as well as the mother's maiden surname.

- The Vietnamese custom of putting the surname first, then the middle name and the given name last.

- The movement among African Americans to confirm pride in their cultural heritage by using names from their homeland rather than names whose historical roots are traced back to the days of slavery.

- The tendency of third and fourth generation descendants of immigrants to have Americanized first names coupled with their traditional family surname.

Name Interview Worksheet

1.   What is your name?

2.   How do you feel about your name? What do you like about it? What don't you like about it?

3.   What do you know about how you got that name? Were you named after someone else? Who named you?

4.   Are there members in your family who have the same name?

5.   Do you have any classmates who have the same name as yours?

6.   Are there any famous people who have the same name as yours?

7.   In what ways are you like or not like these other people who have the same name?

8.   Does your name have any other meaning?

9.   Was your name originally in another language? How do you say it in the other language? What does your name mean in this other language?

10.   If you could pick a different name, what name would you want?

11.   What do you like about that name?

12.   Native Americans often have names that describe something about them or compare them to something in nature. Whispering Elk, Sitting Bull, Running Deer are examples. If you could make up such a name for yourself, what would it be?

7

A Sandwich By Any Other Name

> *It is in part the very uniqueness of every individual that makes him, not only a member of a family, race, nation or class, but a human being.*
>
> –Helen Merrel Lynd

Purpose

A hungry Eighteenth Century nobleman requested a snack. The resulting concoction, consisting of two pieces of bread with a slice of meat between them, has become identified ever since with the Earl of Sandwich.

This is probably the most familiar example of an **eponym:** words in common usage that were once the names of actual persons.

The purpose of this activity is for students to increase their sense of pride by considering how their names might live beyond them as a designation for something that people find useful.

Procedure

1.   Hand out copies of the Eponyms Worksheet* and have students connect the names in column 1 with the items in column 2.

   You may want to allow the students to work cooperatively in small groups to make the accurate identification of items. Dictionaries and encyclopedias may also be made available for students to research the items that are unknown to them.

---

* The eponyms used in this activity were suggested by an article, "The Word as Person" by Don Farrant Sky Magazine, Halsey Publishing Co.: 1992.

2.   Next, have the students consider something with which they might like to have their name connected. It may be something that does not yet exist that the student could imagine creating or something that already exists but the student makes unique in some way.

Suggest that the students consider which name or part of their name (first, middle, or last name) they would use as the eponym.

3.   Move the students into small groups to share their answers.

Variations

Use a television talk show format to interview students on how their names got to be associated with the particular thing they chose.

The students could also put together a newsletter in which they could report on the many contributions of the class as reflected in the number of things named after them.

This could be made into a craft project where students draw or create the item to which their name would be connected.

Eponym Worksheet Answers

1. c   6. d
2. e   7. j
3. b   8. g
4. a   9. h
5. f   10. i

Eponyms Worksheet

Connect names in column 1 with the item in column 2 associated with this person.

Column 1		*Column 2*	
1.	Nellie Melba Australian soprano	a.	railroad car with sleeping quarters
2.	James T. Brundell Seventh Earl of Cardigan British General	b.	loose woman's trouser gathered at the knee
3.	Amelia Bloomer American feminist	c.	thin slices of crisp toast
4.	George M. Pullman American industrialist	d.	alphabetical characters represented by raised dots used by sightless people
5.	Jeanne Antoinette Poisson the Marquise de Pompadour	e.	collarless jacket opened down the front
6.	Louis Braille Frenchman	f.	the style of dressing one's hair high over the forehead
7.	Robert W. Bunsen German professor	g.	refusal to do business with a person or company in order to bring about a settlement
8.	Captain Charles Boycott Irish land agent	h.	a horse race such as the one in Kentucky
9.	Edward Smith Stanley 12th Earl of Derby	i.	a unit of electrical power
10.	James Watt Scottish engineer	j.	type of gas burner

Bonus Questions:

11.   What did Samuel F.B. Morse invent?   _____

12.   Can you think of any other eponymous words? _____

_____

_____

With what would you like to have your own name associated?

Maybe:

- a type of food

- article of clothing

- game or sport

- new invention

Chapter One   *Suggested Student Readings*

ANDERSON, ELOISE A. *Carlos Goes to School*. New York: Warner, 1973.

AYER, JACQUELINE. *NuDang and His Kite*. New York: Harcourt Brace, 1959.

BALES, CAROL ANN. *Kevin Cloud: Chippewa Boy in the City*. Chicago: Reilly & Lee, 1972.

BATDORF, CAROL. *Tinka: A Day in a Little Girl's Life*. Blaine, WA: Hancock House, 1990.

DEMI. *Liang and the Magic Paintbrush*. New York: Harper & Row, 1982.

HAMILTON, VIRGINIA. *Drylongso*. New York: Harcourt Brace Jovanovich, 1993.

HEAD, BARRY AND JIM SEQUIN. *Who Am I?* Illinois: Hubbard, 1975.

HOFFMAN, MARY AND CAROLINE BINCH. *Amazing Grace*. New York: Dial, 1991.

SAIKI, PATSY SUMIE. *Sachie, a Daughter of Hawaii*. Honolulu, HI: Kisaku, 1977.

SAN SOUCI, ROBERT. *The Legend of Scarface*. New York: Doubleday, 1978.

WOLF, JANET. *Adelaide to Zeke*. New York: Harper & Row, 1977.

CHAPTER TWO

Pride and Joy

Celebrating Self

> *There is a vitality, a life-force, an energy, a quickening that is translated through you into action and because there is only one of you in all of time, this expression is unique. And if you block it, it will never exist through any other medium and be lost.*
>
> —Martha Graham

Introduction

Fourth grade got off to a less than auspicious start. Being tardy on the very first day of school is not the way to win points with a new teacher. Miss Goode, however, was not your typical teacher.

Her reaction to my late arrival was to welcome me warmly. Mentioning that she had my older brother last year, she said she was looking forward to having another Siccone in her class. I felt like I belonged.

For students who completed work before the rest of the class, Miss Goode kept a table of supplementary reading material in the back of the room. I latched on to one of these — a book about American leaders from George Washington to George Washington Carver. A place in me resonated with these stories of greatness and social contribution, and I too wanted to be someone special, to become someone who made a difference.

That book, by the way, is still in my possession. Even though it had been given to Miss Goode by her favorite nephew, she was willing to part with it — a gift to me, her favorite student, on the last day of school. That spirit of being good enough to have great things expected of me — nurtured by my fourth grade teacher — remains with me also.

Chapter Two continues the themes established in the first section — take pride in who you are and enjoy being yourself. Students learn it is okay to love themselves even while they are working on improving things they don't like about themselves.

Favorite Things

> **W**e can only be said to be alive in those moments when our hearts are conscious of our treasures.
>
> —Thornton Wilder

Purpose

This activity works well as an "ice breaker." It allows students to get to know each other better through sharing about things that they like.

Procedure

1. Hand out copies of the Favorite Things Worksheet, or have students brainstorm topics and create their own worksheet.

2. Have students walk around the room interviewing each other by asking their fellow students one of the questions on the worksheet.

3. In each box on the worksheet the student is to write the name of the student interviewed and his/her answer to the question. Each of the nine boxes is to be filled in with the name and answer of a different student.

4. Let the students know that they will have about 10 minutes to complete the activity. Call time when you see that most of the students are finished.

5. Bring the students together in a circle (or divide into smaller groups). Focusing on one student at a time, ask the rest of the group what they learned about this student. Continue around class until each student's favorite things have been revealed.

Variation

If you want to reduce the amount of time required to do this activity, you can divide the class into three teams of approximately ten students each and have them interview just the classmates on their team. The sharing would be done in their teams as well.

Favorite Things Worksheet

1. Name _____ Favorite Color _____	2. Name _____ Favorite Food _____	3. Name _____ Favorite Music _____
4. Name _____ Favorite Book _____	5. Name _____ Favorite Subject in School _____	6. Name _____ Favorite Hobby _____
7. Name _____ Favorite TV Program _____	8. Name _____ Favorite Family Activity _____	9. Name _____ Favorite Thing to Do with Friends _____

9

If You Were . . .

If one is lucky, a solitary fantasy can totally transform one million realities.

—Maya Angelou

Purpose

This activity serves as a good warm-up exercise and energizer. It helps students get to know their fellow classmates at a safe, low level of self-disclosure.

Student answers can be studied for patterns that relate to their self-identity by looking to see if there are common characteristics among the chosen items.

Procedure

1. Hand out copies of the If You Were . . . Worksheet.

2. Have students mill around the room interviewing each other. For example, "If you were an animal, what animal would you be? What characteristic of that animal do you like?"

3. Each box on the worksheet is to be filled out about a different student so that nine classmates are interviewed during the process.

4. Inform the class that they have about 10 minutes to do the activity.

5. When the students are finished, bring them together in a circle and have them share what they discovered about each other.

If You Were . . . Worksheet

1. Name _____ Animal _____ Characteristic _____	**2. Name** _____ Color _____ Characteristic _____	**3. Name** _____ Song _____ Characteristic _____
4. Name _____ Musical Instrument _____ Characteristic _____	**5. Name** _____ Room in a House _____ Characteristic _____	**6. Name** _____ Type of Food _____ Characteristic _____
7. Name _____ Car _____ Characteristic _____	**8. Name** _____ Famous Person _____ Characteristic _____	**9. Name** _____ Folktale Character _____ Characteristic _____

The students can brainstorm other topics and create their own worksheet.

10

I Just Wrote to Say, "I Love You"

> **W**e all feel more beautiful when we are loved. And when you have self-love you are always beautiful.
>
> —Alice Walker

Purpose

To support students in remembering to love themselves even when it may be hard to do so.

Materials

An envelope for each student
A piece of paper (preferably lined) or stationery for each student
Pens or pencils

Procedure

1.   Ask students to think of a time when they felt really sad—when they were angry, depressed, disappointed, jealous, embarrassed, or all these at once.

2.   Then, brainstorm with your students ways in which they were able to snap out of these negative feelings — they listened to music, someone told them a joke, they got a hug, they read a fun book, and so forth.

3.   Now ask them to imagine some time in the future when they might get into that frame of mind again: when they might think they are feeling so sad they'll never be happy again; when they might start believing they are really rotten and useless; when they are in such trouble they can't see any way out; when they wish the earth would just open up and swallow them!

4. Ask the students to consider what they would need to hear to snap out of the negative frame of mind. What reminders, examples, sayings, stories, and so on would put them back in touch with the fact that they are lovable and capable persons?

5. Once they know what they would need to hear, tell them to write themselves each a personal letter—to be opened and read only when they need it.

6. You might suggest that in their letter they remind themselves that they knew there was a possibility they would feel this way some time. And that there is another way of feeling. Ask them to write whatever they know will soothe them, humor them, and get them back in touch with loving themselves.

7. When they have finished their letters, have your students put them in the envelopes, seal them, and mark them TOP SECRET. Recommend that they put them in a special place and save them until needed.

11

"I Love Myself Even When . . ."

> *Friendship with oneself is all-important, because without it one cannot be friends with anyone else in the world.*
>
> —Eleanor Roosevelt

Purpose

This activity lets students experience loving themselves unconditionally by distinguishing between (1) who they *are* and (2) what they *do* or *have*. In this activity, they acknowledge themselves for all the things they like about themselves. Then they consider what they don't like and find ways to accept themselves anyway.

Materials

Art paper (12 x 18 inches)
Colored markers or crayons
Paste or glue

Procedure

1.   Have each student bring a recent photograph of him- or herself to class.

2.   Read the story, *Mama, Do You Love Me ?* by Barbara M. Joose (San Francisco: Chronicle Books, 1991).

3.   Give each student a piece of art paper and ask him or her to glue the picture in the center of the paper.

4.   Now provide the following instructions:

    Next to your picture, with a colored marking pen or crayon—pick a color that you like—write or draw one thing about yourself that you like, appreciate, or are proud of. Consider different aspects of yourself—your appearance, your talents, your personality, and so on.

Now turn the paper over. Using a marker of a color you don't like, write or draw one thing you dislike about yourself.

Turn back to the front side. Write (or draw) another thing you like about yourself. (Use a color you like.) Then turn the paper over and write a second thing you dislike about yourself. (Use a color you don't like.)

Continue to write (or draw) things you like about yourself on the picture side and things you dislike about yourself on the opposite side, using the appropriate colored marking pens for each item." This could be kept simpler for younger children by limiting it to one or two things they like/dislike, and by giving them the frame sentence: "I love myself when . . ."

After you have written all the negative things about yourself you can think of, read each criticism and then write above it the words, "I love myself even when . . ."

You are acknowledging that you are lovable with or without your faults; the faults are related to what you have or what you do, not who you are. You, the person, are completely worthy of being loved.

5.   Have students get into a group. Ask them to take turns showing their pictures to the group and explaining the things they like and don't like about themselves.

6.   When everyone in each group has finished, you may have them hang their pictures, with the positive side showing, on the bulletin board. Otherwise, instruct them to take them home and hang them up.

Note: *This activity invites a higher degree of self-disclosure than the earlier ones. Let students know that it is up to them how much personal information they want to share during this and all future activities. They are in control of their answers, and are always free to pass.*

12

To Change The Things I Can

> *G*rowth itself
> contains the germ
> of happiness.
>
> — Pearl Buck

Purpose

In the previous activity, "I Love Myself Even When," students identified some things they like about themselves as well as some things they don't. This exercise, geared for older students, helps them realize that while there may be some personal traits that cannot be changed, other characteristics are in our power to control and improve.

Procedure

1. Have students refer to their drawings done for the earlier activity "I Love Myself Even When," using the side of things they don't like about themselves as a starting point.

2. Hand out copies of the Worksheet, To Change The Things I Can.

3. Now, give them the following instructions:

    Looking at the back of your drawing where you wrote or drew pictures of things you don't like about yourself, pick those aspects of yourself that you feel you can change and write them in the first column of your worksheet.

    Any aspects of yourself that you feel you cannot change, please put down in the second column. If you are not sure whether you can change a particular characteristic, put it in the third column. Are there any questions? Is there anyone who is unclear or doesn't understand the instructions?

4.   After the students have had time to fill out the top part of their worksheet, have them get together with a partner, in small groups or as a full class to discuss the process so far.

5.   Next conduct a full class discussion on how people can change things they don't like about themselves. Using your own worksheet as an example and/or asking a couple of students to volunteer their answers, pick a trait that can be changed and have your students brainstorm ways of producing the desired change. For example:

Something I want to change
    — Shyness

Things I can do
    — Tell myself I'm okay.
    — Practice talking more when I'm with friends.
    — Force myself to raise my hand more often in class.
    — Really do my homework so I feel confident about what I have to say.
    — Talk with someone who is more outgoing and ask them for advice.

6.   Ask students to fill in the bottom of their worksheets.

Pick one area that you want to work on changing. List some things you can do this week to start to make the change.

7.   Have students return to their partner, small group or full group to share their action plans. If they need help thinking of more things they can do this week, let them ask for ideas from their classmates.

8.   Set aside time later in the week to have students share their progress in making the changes they have identified.

To Change The Things I Can Worksheet

Things I Can Change	Things I Can Not Change	Not Sure
_____	_____	_____
_____	_____	_____
_____	_____	_____
_____	_____	_____
_____	_____	_____
_____	_____	_____

Something I want to change _____

Things I will do this week

_____

_____

_____

_____

13

Relaxing At The Beach

> ***M****ay you live all the days of your life.*
>
> —Jonathan Swift

Purpose

This activity is an introduction to a relaxation technique that students can use to calm down and to reduce stress.

Materials

Tape player and cassette with ocean wave sound

Procedure

1.   Introduce the activity to your students by saying:

> *Have you ever felt so nervous that your body shook? Have you ever been so grumpy that your friends turned away? Have you ever been too tired to do your schoolwork? I'm going to show you a safe and healthy way of controlling your shaking body, grumpy attitude, and tired body. You will feel more energy and happiness, and be more relaxed. The more you practice this method, the better you'll get at it.*

Teacher gives personal examples and allows students to respond to some of the questions.

2.   Have all students clear their desks and sit back in their chairs with knees forward and feet flat on the floor. Hands may be in a relaxed position on the desk or in the lap. Leave window blinds open and turn off lights. Be sure the room temperature is cool and the environment quiet. Demonstrate position for students before beginning exercise.

3.   Now explain:

We are going on an imaginary field trip to the beach.

Turn on the tape of ocean sounds.

4.   Tell students they may practice this relaxation technique with their eyes open if they feel uncomfortable keeping them closed. Be sure all external noises are kept to a minimum.

5.   Slowly and calmly read the following instructions to class:

Close your eyes [optional], take a deep breath and just relax. [Pause]

Now, pretend that you are at the beach. The weather is perfect. The sun is shining and the warm air feels good on your skin. As you walk on the beach, barefooted, the soles of your feet glide easily through the warm grains of sand. You hear the voices of seagulls calling to each other. A cool breeze passes by and all your worries disappear. You slowly sit down on the soft sand and bury your hands in it. Soon you find yourself drawing pictures in the sand and pouring sand over your feet. As the surf comes in and out you feel relaxed and full of energy.

Now think about all the good things you really are.

Repeat these positive sentences to yourself after me:

I like myself.

I am happy.

I am in perfect health.

I have full control of myself.

I am using more and more of my mind each day.

Every day, in every way, I am growing better, better, and better.

Now, open your eyes slowly and feel yourself relaxed and full of energy.

6.   Class discussion. Ask:

How do you feel now compared with before the relaxation exercise? What was the beach like? When and why could you pretend to go to the beach again?

Follow-Up Activity

Have students draw their beach scene.

14

Stress Stoppers

The sense of existence is the great happiness.

—Benjamin Disraeli

Purpose

One of the most common examples of the physical effects of stress on the body is known as the "fight or flight" syndrome. If you were in a jungle and came upon a tiger, your body would automatically furnish a powerful surge of adrenaline and send a supply of adrenaline and cholesterol into the bloodstream to help you fight the tiger or flee it. When the danger passed, you would fall to the ground exhausted. The adrenaline would have been used up (metabolized) and you could rest.

Unfortunately, humans can trigger this same physiological reaction with negative thoughts, fear, or tension. The adrenaline and cholesterol race around the bloodstream, but when we don't have a clear enemy to fight, we ourselves become victims. In fact, the symptoms of a stress attack resemble the warning signs of a heart attack.

Three effective stress reduction techniques are taught in this lesson: relaxation, "stop thought," and the transformation of negative messages into positive ones. These techniques can reduce or eliminate stress before it becomes damaging to the body.

Procedure

1.   Begin the lesson by saying:

   Today we are going to learn three techniques to stop stress. Imagine you are all by yourself in a haunted house at midnight. It's dark, you hear creaking sounds, the wind is whistling through an open window, and a door keeps opening and closing. What happens to your heart, your breath, your skin? What thoughts do you have?

2.   Elicit responses from students (heart beats fast, skin is cold/clammy, and so forth). Then say:

> *Sometimes in real life when we are afraid or worried about something, we feel the same reactions in our body.*

Elicit examples of stressful situations from students.

> *Today we are going to practice three techniques to help reduce that tension or stress.*

3.   Have the whole class practice relaxation steps.

   a.   Breathe from your diaphragm.
   b.   Take in a deep breath for four seconds.
   c.   Hold it for four seconds.
   d.   Breathe out for four seconds.

4.   Explain the "stop thought" technique:

> *When negative thoughts begin, imagine a stop sign or say "stop!" to yourself. Then take a few deep breaths from your diaphragm. Hold your breath for a moment or two and exhale slowly, softly, and steadily. At the same time, tell your body to go limp or melt.*

Then have a student suggest a negative thought, such as "I'm going to fail the test" or "Everybody is going to laugh at me when we play volleyball." Ask the class to use the stop-thought and deep-breathing techniques. Do several times with different thoughts.

> *Finally, change the negative thought to a positive one. Instead of saying, "I'm going to fail the test," say, "I will pass the test. I'll ask my friend to help me study for it." Now do the whole process. Use the stop-thought, breathe deeply and relax, and change the negative thought into a positive statement.*

5.   Ask students for examples of negative thoughts turned into positive statements. Chart some of the more common examples to give the students tools for future negative situations.

6.   Chart and post stress reduction steps for student use.

Follow-Up Activities

1. Use the technique during the next few weeks if negative situations occur in the classroom or on the yard.

2. Ask students to report orally or in writing about successful experiences with the stress reduction techniques.

3. Have students share the three techniques with their parents, younger siblings, or playmates.

15

Highlights of My Life

> **W**hen I was born, I was so surprised I couldn't talk for a year and a half.
>
> —Gracie Allen

Purpose

One's life experiences make up a significant part of one's identity. The aim of this activity is for students to reflect on the major events of their lives, and consider how these events contributed to making them unique.

Materials

Drawing supplies, such as pencils, crayons or colored markers

Procedure

1.   Hand out copies of the Highlights of My Life Worksheet.

2.   Have students draw a picture in each frame representing a highlight event in their lives. Ask them to recall moments when they felt special or felt especially happy or successful.

3.   Students can then get into groups of six or eight and take turns sharing their highlights.

Highlights of My Life Worksheet — I

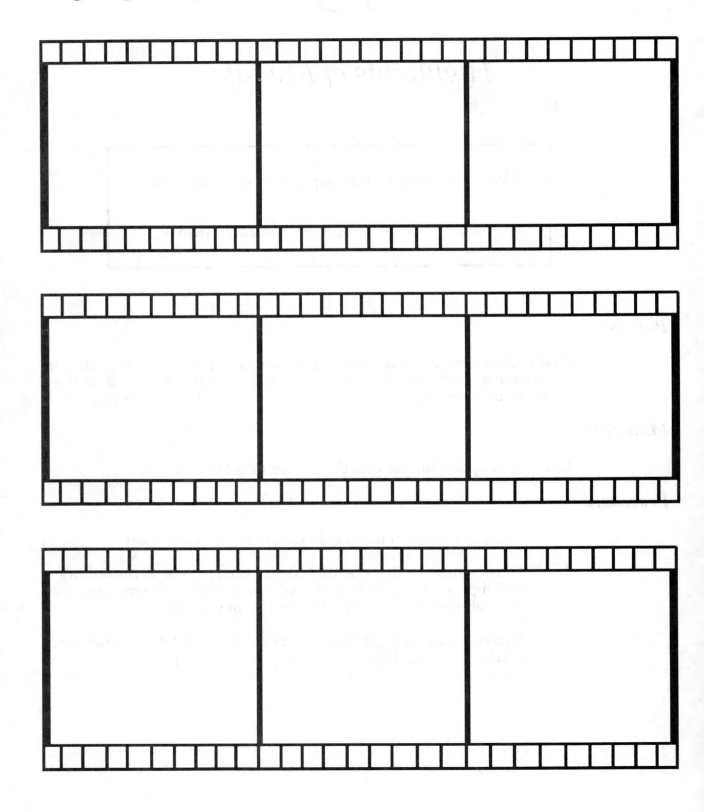

16

Award Winners

> ***S**ilent gratitude isn't very much use to anyone.*
>
> —G.B. Stern

Purpose

Most students are probably aware of the numerous awards shows on television, such as the Oscars, the Grammies, and the MTV Awards. This activity is an opportunity for students to acknowledge the positive qualities that they recognize in their classmates. It completes the sequence of activities on names by having each award named for the student who receives it. You can also record this activity and play it at a parent meeting or school assembly.

Note: Please read the next activity, Play TV, before doing this one in case you want to integrate the two.

Procedure

1.   Divide the class into small groups.

2.   Give each group the names of five other students in the class to acknowledge at the awards ceremony.

3.   Ask the students when they get the names not to let anyone know whose acknowledgments they are going to do. A surprise will make it more fun.

4.   Instruct each group to take the names one at a time.

Consider the things about the person that you like, admire, and appreciate; those things that make the person special.

5.   Now that they have a list of qualities and contributions for which to acknowledge the person, direct each group of students to think of a way of summarizing in the form of a special award what that person has done for the group. For example, there might be a person who gets the *thoughtfulness award* for always being kind to people, helping people who are having problems, and so on. Or there might be a *good humor award* for a person who lightens up heavy situations, and is always good for a laugh.

6.   Hand out copies of the Awards Certificate Worksheet and have the students complete one certificate for each of the names they received. The award is named after the student who will receive it, and the person's special attribute is filled in on the line provided. Encourage students to decorate each certificate with colors and designs that make it personal to the recipient.

7.   When all the groups are finished, they are to bring their awards to the awards ceremony (class circle). You, as master of ceremonies, will call on each group to make their awards. If they want to, they can pretend they are Oscar presenters and call for "The envelope, please." That might add to the fun. Be sure that each group does a good job of explaining and displaying the award and letting the winner feel the full sincerity of their acknowledgment.

You may want to discuss how to receive compliments graciously.

8.   Close with a discussion using questions such as:

What award did you receive at the awards ceremony?

How did it feel to receive this compliment?

Do you ever acknowledge yourself for these good qualities? If you don't, take the time to do that now.

Follow-Up Activity

Students can list people in their lives who deserve to be acknowledged for the things they have done for the students in the past month. The students could then be encouraged to make awards for these people or in some other creative way acknowledge these people for their contributions.

Awards Worksheet

_____

AWARD
is presented to

_____

for

_____

_____

_____

Awards Worksheet

MALIKAH

AWARD
is presented to

Malikah Brown

for`
Being a Special Friend

Part I — Key Learnings

- I am somebody special.

- It is okay for me to say, "I love myself." This is not bragging. It is knowing that I am worthwhile.

- My being here is important.

- I love myself even when I do things that I do not like.

- I belong here.

- I was born for a good reason.

- I am unique.

- I was born with special gifts and talents and it is my responsibility to do something with these.

- I have something of value to share.

Part I—Teacher Checklist
Valuing Myself and All My Students

Note: At the end of each of the four parts of this book, a Teacher Checklist is provided. Please take a minute to reflect on the extent to which you have integrated the lessons of these two chapters.

❑   Do I think that teaching is an important profession?

❑   Do I have confidence in my ability to find ways of being successful with all students?

❑   Am I able to love myself even when I do things that are not successful?

❑   Are my relationships healthy and do I feel capable of loving and being loved?

❑   Do I feel powerful in being able to direct my life toward my goals?

❑   Have I ever been at the receiving end of some form of discrimination, and have I been able to make peace with these incidents?

❑   Am I open–minded enough to accept other point of views as being equally valid?

❑   Do I pay attention and give positive feedback to all students equally?

❑   Am I willing to pay closer attention to my interaction with students; noticing which ones I am more or less comfortable with, which ones I expect the most from, which ones I call on the most, praise and encourage the most and so forth?

❑   If I discover cultural, ethnic or gender biases, am I willing to correct these?

Chapter Two   *Suggested Student Readings*

ADOFF, ARNOLD. *Black Is Brown Is Tan*. New York: Harper and Row, 1973.

DR. SEUSS. *My Book About Me*. New York: Random House, 1969.

ETS, MARIA HALL. *Bad Boy, Good Boy*. New York: Crowell, 1967.

GREENFIELD, ELOISE. *Daydreamers*. New York: Dial, 1981.

JOOSSE, BARBARA M. AND BARBARA LAVALLEE. *Mama, Do You Love Me?* San Francisco: Chronicle Books, 1991.

LEE, JEANNE M. *Ba-Nam*. New York: Henry Holt & Co., 1987.

NIXON, JOAN L. *The Gift*. New York: Macmillan, 1983.

PAEK, M. *Aekyung's Dream*. Chicago: Children's Press, 1978.

PITTMAN, HELENA. *The Gift of the Willows*. Minneapolis, MN: Carolrhoda, 1988.

POLITI, LEO. *The Nicest Gift*. New York: Scribner's, 1973.

RINGGOLD, FAITH. *Tar Beach*. New York: Crown, 1991.

SEED, JENNY. *Ntombi's Song*. Boston: Beacon Press, 1987.

SHAH, INDRIES. *World Tales*. New York: Harcourt Brace Jovanovich, 1979.

UCHIDA, YOSHIKO. *Makoto, The Smallest Boy*. New York: Thomas Y. Crowell Co., 1970.

WALKER, ALICE AND CATHERINE DEETER. *Finding the Green Stone*. New York: Harcourt Brace Jovanovich, 1991.

PART II

RESPECT FOR OTHERS AND INTERDEPENDENCE

Freedom to Be We

Nobody, but nobody can make it here alone.

—Maya Angelou

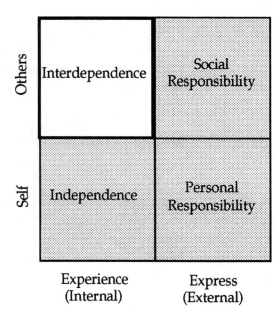

CHAPTER THREE

Social Identity

Roots from Which to Grow

> *To be rooted is perhaps the most important and least recognized need of the human soul.*
>
> —Simone Weil

Introduction

Families—no matter what size or shape—are the basic units of love and support for children. The ratio of nuclear families in the U.S. households has dropped from 40% in 1970, to 26% in 1990, according to the Bureau of Census. This indicates that three out of four children in today's schools come from a home with a family configuration other than mom, dad and kids all living under the same roof. Schools must reach out to families and get them involved in their youngsters' education. In order for this to happen, members of the family need to feel welcome and wanted.

The activities in this chapter invite students to share about their families so that they feel that their life experiences are legitimate and that they indeed belong in this classroom. A sense of belonging, a feeling of being connected with the group is an essential ingredient to healthy self–esteem.

By virtue of what is and is not included in the curriculum, schools play a critical role in establishing what knowledge, values and life experiences are deemed worthwhile. Students whose culture is reflected in their school will feel validated; their "cultural capital"* will be increased. Conversely, ethnic groups who are not included feel devalued and their cultural capital depleted. Students in this situation are faced with the dilemma of either rejecting their own culture and embracing that of the school's in order to succeed, or negating the value of school in order to protect their self-pride. This is a choice no one should have to make.

Similar to the theory of cultural capital is the "poker chip" analogy of self-esteem. The idea is that students who have a history of previous success and positive acknowledgment are in possession of a sizable stack of chips — a psychological bank account of self-valuing experiences from which to draw in dealing with life's challenges. If they take a risk at this point and don't succeed, the one or two chips they loose are not significant given their total number. They are able to stay in the game.

On the other hand, students who have had few opportunities to experience success and receive positive recognition have a great deal to lose given that one or two chips may be all they have with which to play. Dropping out of the game may seem the only logical thing to do. Schools have a responsibility to empower students by giving them a chance to build up their self-esteem "chips" and to increase their cultural capital.

---

* For further discussion of the idea of "cultural capital" see Pierre Bourdien, "The Forms of Capital," in *Handbook of Theory and Research for the Sociology of Education*, ed. John G. Richardson (New York: Greenwood Press, 1986).

17

Willkommen, Bienvenidos, Welcome

Background

Language plays a critical role in our culture identity. It is how we express ourselves. Beyond words, language communicates a certain style or personality. Language embodies a people's history and geography. It has texture and color, rhythm and tempo. Language can convey a shared perspective toward life and a sense of humor. Many of these elements can get lost in translation.

Much has been written about bilingual education. Controversies revolve around whether it is effective or not, and whether or not lack of proficiency in English is the major reason for the academic failure of language–minority students.

The purpose of bilingual education is also debated. Is the objective for students to learn English as quickly as possible because this is the key to equal opportunity? Is the point to teach academic subjects in the students' primary language so that they do not fall behind in subject matter content while they are learning English? Is the vision or should the vision be true bilingualism, biliteracy—a nation of people that are linguistically competent and thus better able to function in the world—a world of many languages and cultures?

However these debates get resolved, the fact remains that building a child's self–esteem in today's multicultural classroom has got to include a sensitivity to the students' linguistic heritage.

Students should be encouraged to use their primary language around school:

- as part of the learning process (for example, in cooperative learning groups made up of students from the same ethnic group on at least some occasions)

- in elective subjects and extracurricular activities

- in writing for school newspapers and other official school communications

- during assemblies, award presentations and other schoolwide functions.

The following activity is one step in this direction.

Purpose

The purpose of this exercise is to create a welcoming classroom for all students, especially those for whom English is not their primary language.

Procedure

1. Determine the native languages of the students in your class, and learn how to say "Welcome" in each language. You may want to include other languages that your students will find in their community, or will be studying later in school. You may also want to ask your students what other languages interest them.

    In addition to the word "Welcome" you might also want to teach the children a few other words or phrases in each language such as "Thank you."

2. Prepare a large banner to hang in front of the room with the word, "Welcome" on it. Each day use a different language.

3. Have the students practice saying the word during the morning class meeting or My Circle of Friends time (Activity 28). When one student has finished sharing, he or she passes the turn to the next student in the circle by saying "Welcome" and that student's name.

4. If visitors come into your classroom during this time, have the students greet the person by saying "Welcome" in the language of the day.

5. Use other simple words from the focus language throughout the day whenever possible.

6. You may want to read with your students the book, *Welcome Roberto! Bienvenido, Roberto!* by Mary Senfozo (Chicago: Follett, 1969).

CHINESE	- *Huan Yin*	*Xie-Xie*
ENGLISH	- *Welcome*	*Thank You*
FRENCH	- *Bienvenu*	*Merci*
GERMAN	- *Willkommen*	*Danke Schön*
ITALIAN	- *Benvenuti*	*Grazie*
JAPANESE	- *Irrashaimase*	*Arigato*
PORTUGUESE	- *Boas–vindas*	*Obrigado*
SPANISH	- *Bienvenidos*	*Gracias*
VIETNAMESE	- *Chao Mung*	*Cám On*

18

We Are More Alike Than Different

> *May we open to a deeper understanding and a genuine love and caring for the multitude of faces, who are none other than ourself.*
>
> — Wendy Egyoku Nakao

Purpose

Students will become more aware and accepting of each other by learning things that they have in common as well as things that are different.

Materials

Prepare a "Same Game" sheet for student use. Items can be revised, shortened, or expanded for the interests and experiences of the class.

Procedure

1. Start by saying:

    Now we are going to play a game where we discover things we have in common with other people in the class. It's called "The Same Game."

2. Give students copies of the sheet and instruct them to walk around the room and ask one another the questions that are appropriate, such as "In what month were you born?"

3. Tell students to fill in their sheets with the names of other students with whom they have things in common and the things they share.

4. You may want to set up your guidelines for this activity according to your classroom's discipline policy concerning walking around and talking.

For example:
    a. Walk, don't run.
    b. Talk quietly.
    c. Stay on task.
    d. When finished, go back to your seat and sit quietly.

5.   After the students have filled in their papers, encourage them to share their findings in a class discussion. Conclude with a discussion on the topic: "What did you learn about our likenesses and differences?"

Follow-Up Activities:

1.   Have students chart the months in which they were born or some other item.

2.   Have students line up to indicate a like or dislike. For example, tell the class:

> *I will ask about things that you will either feel strongly about one way or the other or that you may be somewhere in the middle about. When I ask, decide how you feel and then stand in a line, all facing me, according to how you feel about it. For example, I may say: "People who like chocolate best stand to the right, people who like vanilla best stand to the left and those who don't feel strongly either way stand in the middle."*

a. Ask about items, one at a time.

    Examples: People who love pizza—people who hate pizza.

                   People who enjoy cooking—people who dislike cooking.

                   People who wish it would rain more—people who wish it would never rain.

                   People who would rather go to the ocean—people who would rather go to the mountains.

b. Give about a minute for people to line up for each issue. Emphasize that children should think for themselves and not wait to see where a friend is standing. Allow quiet talking about their opinions, such as "I love pizza, too" or "I didn't know you liked the mountains!"

The Same Game Worksheet

Name_____

Find someone else who:	Things in Common	Name
Ate the same thing for dinner last night.		
Was born in the same month as you.		
Has the same favorite color as you.		
Has a middle name like yours.		
Is wearing the same color socks.		
Saw the same TV show last night.		
Feels the same about spiders.		
Wants (has) the same kind of pet.		
Has the same number of brothers and sisters.		
Has the same favorite food.		

19

The Joy of Eating

*F*ood is the most primitive form of comfort.

—Sheilah Graham

A good cook is like a sorceress who dispenses happiness.

—Elsa Schiaparelli

Background

Food is at the heart of most cultures. It often embodies the heritage of a race, traces historical and geographic influences over time, reflects a style, an aesthetic, and the taste — literally as well as figuratively — of a particular culture. It is hard to imagine Italians without pasta, Mexicans without tortillas, Asians without rice and Americans without apple pie.

American food, however, is certainly more than just apple pie. Many foods that are considered American have origins that can be traced to other lands. Peanuts came from South America, for instance. Other examples are potatoes from the Andes via Ireland, oranges picked in Asia, traded to Africa and the Middle East by Arabs, and brought here from the Mediterranean countries.

Pumpkin pie blends the English concept of pie with Native American pumpkin and Asian spices like cinnamon and nutmeg. "Puffed" cereal also originated in the colonial days when English housewives served Native American popcorn with sugar and cream for breakfast.

American food customs are derived from all parts of the word: Consider Chinese–style chicken salad, Cajun–spiced French fries, teriyaki hamburgers and Mexican Pizza. Today's grocery stores are stocked with the necessary ingredients to prepare every type of food imaginable.

Purpose

This activity helps students identify with their cultural roots and take pride in its culinary contributions.

Procedure

1.   Ask students to identify the person at home who cooks their favorite meal.

2.   Give students the assignment of interviewing this person to find out as much as possible about the food they enjoy.

Either prepare a list of questions in advance and hand these out to the students as a way of structuring the interview, or together with the students, brainstorm possible questions to ask such as:

- How long have you been cooking this type of food?

- How did you learn how to prepare it?

- How long has the recipe been in the family?

- How did our people come to this type of cooking?

Note: *You may want to expand this activity to have students go to the library to do more research on how food traditions evolved in their culture.*

3.   Have students bring in a copy of the recipe for their favorite meal.

Students could also bring in a photograph of their favorite meal or do an illustration of part of the recipe.

4.   Make copies of each of the recipes and illustrations and bind these together into booklets so that every student has a complete set of recipes.

Note: *As a class project, these recipe books could be sold to raise money to cover the cost of duplicating and binding. Profits could be used to help finance a field trip or some other activity. (See Team Problem Solving, Activity 56, for a possible way of structuring this.)*

Also, this "business venture" could be used to teach math concepts.

If feasible, students could actually prepare some of the recipes in class, or a Multicultural Food Fare or potluck could be held where family members are invited to bring in dishes to share with each other. Back–to –School Night, holiday celebrations or graduation would be particular good times for such an activity.

When snacks are made available to students, consider ways of providing nutritional food reflective of many cultures.

20

My Own Culture

---

*O*ur mothers and grandmothers, some of them; moving to music not yet written.

—Alice Walker

Background*

Many cultures have their own folklore regarding the importance of a new year with particular customs that are intended to ensure good fortune, prosperity, happiness and longevity.

The Ecuadorian New Year is celebrated on December 31, by families creating dolls out of old rags representing the old year. On New Year's Eve the figures are placed on decorated chairs. Everyone pins their resolutions for the New Year on these dolls as the children sing and dance. At midnight the figures are removed as the New Year begins.

Chinese New Year occurs later in January or in February. Families gather together, houses are cleaned, tools repaired, clothes mended and debts paid: all symbolic of completing the past to get ready for a new beginning. Bright red, the color of good fortune, is seen everywhere. Evil spirits are scared away by firecrackers and the Dancing Dragon who brings good wishes.

Vietnamese New Year (Tet) is in the spring. Everything and everyone is prepared for the New Year. As with the Chinese, houses are repainted, furniture cleaned and new clothes are worn.

---

* The background information was adapted from *Children of the Rainbow—First Grade,* Board of Education of The City of New York, 1991, and "Ring in the New Year with Old Customs", by Marina Cianci in *The San Francisco Chronicle*, Dec. 30, 1992.

At midnight, families go to the temple to give thanks. Flowers and branches from fruit trees are used to symbolize prosperity and happiness. People visit friends, give gifts and feast during this spring festival of reunion and renewal.

Some **Native American** tribes celebrated their New Year during the summer in late July or early August when the corn was ripe and the fruits and vegetables were ready to eat.

At this time, family ties were renewed, new law's made, past mistakes forgiven, and all the people of the tribe reflected on the importance of getting along together.

Old fires were put out, new ones were lighted and the Green Corn Dance was celebrated.

Jewish New Year (Rosh Hashanah) in the fall, is a serious holy day that is greeted with a quiet and solemn heart. Sweet foods are served signifying a sweet new year ahead.

Many other cultures have New Year customs that involve food as part of the symbolism.

In Japan, Toshidoshi soba (" year crossover ") noodles are eaten for wealth and long life.

Portuguese eat a dozen raisins or pomegranate seeds—good luck for each month of the year—and the Spanish use grapes for the same purpose.

An Italian custom is eating lentils symbolizing money, and cotechino (a type of pork sausage) symbolizing richness.

The Dutch have their oliebollen—doughnuts, and Greeks have their vasilopita — a wreath of decorated sweet bread with a golden coin hidden inside for good fortune.

In the Southern U.S., rice and black-eyed peas eaten on New Year's Day is thought to bring good luck.

Purpose

This activity will help students appreciate what constitutes a culture, and will engender a greater sense of pride in their culture.

Procedure

1. Write the word, CULTURE, on the board and ask students to brainstorm what they think of when they think of culture.

    You may need to do some coaching such as:

    Teacher: "When I say Chinese culture, what do you think of?"

    Student: "Chinese food."

    Teacher: "Good. So food is one aspect of culture."

    Teacher: "What do you think of when I say "Mexican?"

    Student: "Mariachi Band."

    Teacher: "So, music and dance are part of culture. Good."

    Teacher: "How about French culture?"

    Student: "A beret" or "Oui, oui."

    Teacher: Yes, clothes and language are part of culture."

    Teacher: What do you think of when I say Russia?"

    Student: "Communism."

    Teacher: "Forms of government and historical events also make up a country's culture.

2. Make the point that one way of understanding *culture* is to see it as the knowledge, ideas and skills that enable a group of people to survive in their environment. Basically all people have essentially the same human needs and wants. How these needs get fulfilled in the context of the group's environment is what constitutes culture.

3. Ask the students to name some things they think all human beings need in order to survive. Record their answers on the board or on butcher paper. "Food," "clothing," "shelter" are typical responses. Refer back to the earlier set of questions for other ideas such as language, art, and government. Continue to ask probing questions to help students identify other needs such as: love / family / friendship; work / economy; meaning of life / religion.

4. Hand out the My Culture Worksheet and have the students fill this out on their own culture. If their heritage is multicultural, they may use a separate sheet for each or combine aspects from all their

cultures on the same sheet. Fill one out yourself and use this as a sample. Answer any questions the students might have. For some of the answers, the students may need to refer back to their cultural group's heritage for unique expressions of clothing and shelter, for example.

5.   Have the students share the answers on their worksheets in pairs or small groups.

6.   End the activity with a full class discussion regarding similarities and variations of the different cultures. You could make a chart on the board or on butcher paper to help focus the discussion.

Human Need	German	Korean	Navajo	Filipino
Food				
Clothing				
Shelter				
Language				
Music/Art/Dance				
Family				
Other				

My Culture Worksheet

Name_____Cultural Groups_____

Food_____
_____
_____

Clothing _____
_____
_____

Shelter_____
_____
_____

Language _____
_____
_____

Music/Art/Dance_____
_____
_____

Customs/Traditions Related to Family _____
_____
_____

Other Unique Characteristics _____
_____
_____

21

The Cultures We Are

> *My race is a line that stretches across ocean and time to link me to the shrines where my grandmother was raised.*
>
> —Kesaya E. Noda

Purpose

This could be done in your classroom or as a school-wide activity. It is meant to celebrate all the various cultures in your school community, and to increase awareness and understanding of these cultures.

Procedure

1.   Begin this activity by reading to your class, *Angel Child, Dragon Child* by Michelle Maria Surat. This delightful book is about a Vietnamese child who is at first teased for being different but then her story inspires a new sense of community at her school.

2.   Brainstorm with your students any questions they have that they would like to ask someone from a different culture. It should, of course, be emphasized that respect for all people of all cultures is essential. Possible areas to explore are included in the previous activity. Also consider:

What customs are particular to your culture?

- *at the birth of a child*
- *when someone dies*
- *at weddings*
- *at birthdays*
- *during holidays*
- *rites of passage (bar mitzvah, Confirmation, and so forth)*

What foods are native to your culture?

What are the common characteristics of the artwork created by people in your culture?

What type of music is usually played at family gatherings?

Are there particular colors that are frequently used in the clothing worn by people in your culture?

What artifacts and crafts are enjoyed by people in your culture?

What is your culture's attitude toward its elders?

What rules of conduct determine acceptance or rejection in your culture?

How important is religion/spirituality in your culture?

How is success defined in your culture?

Who are your culture's heroes and heroines?

Some student-generated questions were:

Are your parents strict or easy?

Where do you get your spending money? Do you get an allowance? How much?

Do your parents expect you to go to college?

Are you likely to work in your family's business?

Can you pick your own clothes?

3. Select the seven questions that have the most interest for the class, and ask the students to bring these home to discuss with their families. Pick a date by when all students will bring in their answers.

    You may want to put the questions onto a worksheet to make it easier for the students. You probably also want to inform the families in advance of the assignment so that they will understand its purpose and won't feel that the school is prying into their family background.

4. Plan with your students how you will share this information with each other or with the entire school. Here are some suggestions:

- Cut construction paper into the shape of balloons. Print the name of the culture and one fact about it on each side of the paper and suspend them all from the ceiling with string so that they hang at student eye-level — a celebration of cultural diversity.

- Print a Multicultural Newsletter with a separate page for each culture containing all the facts collected by the students from that particular culture. Students could illustrate the pages of the newsletter with culturally-related drawings.

- Post a large map of the world and highlight the countries of origin represented by your students. Use Post-it® Notes to display facts about the cultures of the countries.

- Have your class publish "Our Geography Book" or "Our History Book" where the facts about the various cultures can be gathered in textbook-like fashion. Additional research could be done to expand the knowledge of each culture.

- Students could design quizzes that they could give to their classmates on each culture.

5. Conclude this activity with a class discussion about what the students learned. Explore with them the idea that one's culture often influences family patterns and yet no one family can represent an entire culture. Families, like individuals, are unique.

22

Sense Us

> *This country is great because of its accommodations with diversity. The richness of the diversity of this country is a treasure and it's a constant challenge to remain tolerant and respectful of one another.*
>
> —Ruth Bader Ginsburg

Background

In 1790, when the first U.S. census was conducted, the race classifications were white, slave, and other. By 1870, the categories had evolved to include white, colored (black), colored (mulattos), Chinese, and Indian. Two decades later, the distinctions among blacks became more detailed: blacks, mulattos (those with three-eighths to five-eighths "black blood"), quadroons (those with one-quarter black blood), and octoroons (those with one-eighth black blood). This "blood" ratio was later dropped; by 1930, anyone of mixed black and white heritage was put in the "Negro" category.

The current racial and ethnic categories are white, black, Asian/Pacific Islander, American Indian, Hispanic, and other. When told to pick one box, however, people of multiracial backgrounds are faced with a dilemma. As interracial marriages increase—from 310,000 in 1970 to 1.2 million in 1992 (a 365 percent jump)—hundreds of thousands of multiracial children cannot officially claim an identity of their own. Should they pick one parent over the other, check the "other" box, check more than one box—or should the form itself be changed? This is the challenge for your students to address.[*]

---

[*] Statistics contained in the background material for this activity come from "Census Misses the Mark on Race" by Thaai Walker, *San Francisco Chronicle*, July 26, 1993.

Purpose

The purpose of this activity is to validate students who are multiracial or multiethnic by raising issues regarding society's view of people who cross racial lines. By the way, it was not until 1967 that the laws barring interracial marriages were fully repealed.

Procedure

1. Discuss with your students the idea of doing a census, what purpose it serves, and the possible reasons for including race categories. For example, the Voting Rights Act requires that minorities have proportional representation in local government and legislation. So, information regarding the ethnic makeup of the population is essential to ensuring that all people are appropriately represented.

2. Hand out the Sense Us Worksheet and ask the students first to check the box that best describes their racial makeup.

3. Next, explain that each category may be made up of specific sub-groups: Hispanic may include Mexican, Puerto Rican, Cuban, and so forth; Asian might include Korean, Vietnamese, and Taiwanese, as well as Chinese and Japanese; white may include any number of European nationalities; and so forth.

   Have students fill in their cultural makeup in greater detail and indicate the relative percentages.

4. Now, demonstrate how to make a pie chart and have the students draw one that reflects their cultural heritage.

5. You may want to extend this activity to the development of a census of the entire class by calculating the data on each student in a composite chart.

6. Students could also do a schoolwide census by distributing the worksheets to each classroom and compiling the data to form a composite pie chart for the entire student body.

7. In discussing the activity with the students afterwards, make reference to the multiracial category as one that is not included on the actual U.S. census. Ask them how they would feel if they could choose only one of the other boxes.

Sense Us Worksheet

Please check the appropriate box:

❑	White	_____	_____%
❑	Black	_____	_____%
❑	Asian/Pacific Islander	_____	_____%
❑	American Indian	_____	_____%
❑	Hispanic	_____	_____%
❑	Other race	_____	_____%
❑	Multirace	_____	_____%

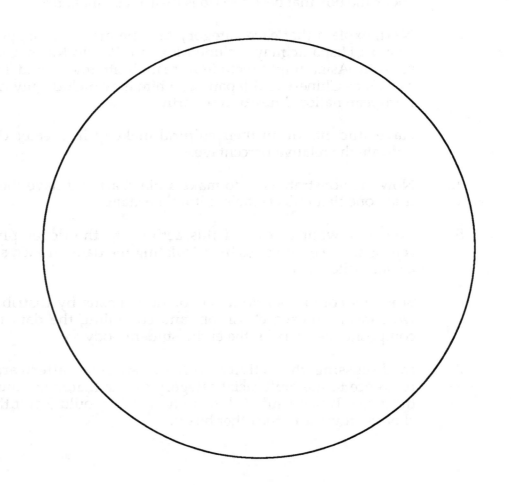

23

Family Values

> *In Vietnam traditional values have deep roots. When the heavy winds blow reeds bend, but when the winds cease, they once again stand straight and tall.*
>
> — Vuong G. Thuy

Purpose

This activity is meant to help students feel a sense of pride for their own families and respect for others' families by furthering understanding and acceptance of nontraditional family structures. With many students coming from families that no longer fit the nuclear-family model of the 1950s, it is important that schools validate the diversity of today's family configurations. Children living with stepparents, grandparents, adopted parents, or gay parents need to feel as comfortable talking about their family life as children living with their biological parents.

Materials

Colored paper cut in the shape of leaves
Art paper
Pens
Glue

Procedure

1. Read to the students, *All Kinds of Families* by Norman Simon (Niles, IL: Whitman Albut & Co., 1976).

2. Write the word "family" on the board and ask your students to help define the term. Consider questions such as:

    What is a family?

What makes someone a member of a family?

When you think of your family, who do you include?

Are there people who you don't see very often who are still part of your family?

Are there people who feel like family but really are not?

What are some things that families do together?

3.   Now, write the word "values" on the board and ask your students' help to define this term.

Consider question such as:

What does the word "values" mean?

If by "values" we mean the most important qualities of someone or something, then what do you value most about your family?

If by "values" we mean our most cherished beliefs or principles, what values did George Washington stand for? How about Mahatma Gandhi, Chief Seattle, Martin Luther King, Mother Teresa, Nelson Mandela, Cesar Chavez, Emperor Hirohito, Shirley Chisholm?

4.   Distribute the art supplies. You may want to have the students work in teams so that they can share some of the materials.

5.   Discuss the idea of a family tree which is used to diagram the lineage of a family and say that we are going to create our own family tree in a somewhat different way.

Rather than tracing the branches from parent-to-parent, generation-by-generation, we are going to display our existing family in the broadest possible terms.

We are also going to identify which values each of our family members represent to us. Values such as:

love	honesty	hardworking
caring	truth	fun
support	integrity	spiritual
understanding	beauty	strength
listening	elegance	success
appreciating	creativity	loyal
sensitivity	intelligent	organized

6.   Instruct the students to start with themselves:

Take a leaf, write your name on it and write one value that you stand for. Paste your leaf somewhere near the center of the page.

Next, think of the family members to whom you feel closest. Write their names on separate leaves and also write down the value that each person represents for you. Glue these leaves on the page near yours.

Continue the activity until you have done a leaf for everyone you consider part of your family.

7.   When the students are finished, have them share their family trees with each other in small groups or as a full class. You may want to post the finished work on a bulletin board, or invite the students to bring them home to share.

Follow-Up Activity

1.   You may want to make this part of a week-long theme on families.

2.   Continue the theme by selecting another one of the books related to families that is developmentally appropriate for your students and that you feel they will enjoy.

For example:

Black Is Brown Is Tan (Adoff, 1973)

Daddy (Caines, 1977)

Martin's Father (Eichler, 1977)

Asha's Mums (Elwin & Paulse, 1990)

Families (Tax, 1981)

Uncle What-Is-It Is Coming To Visit (Willhoite, 1993)

3.   Read the story to the class.

4.   Invite the students to share their thoughts and feelings about the book. Make it safe for them to relate aspects of their own family lives that are similar or different from those pictured without creating any sense of pressure on the part of the children to disclose more than they are comfortable doing.

5.   Continue the theme on subsequent days selecting a different book to be read.

Chapter Three   *Suggested Student Readings*

ADOFF, ARNOLD. *Black Is Brown Is Tan*. New York: Harper & Row, 1973.

ALDEN, J. *A Boy's Best Friend*. Boston: Alyson Press, 1992.

BROWN, F. *The Generous Jefferson Bartleby Jones*. Boston: Alyson Press, 1991.

BROWN, TRICIA. *Chinese New Year*. New York: Henry Holt, 1987.

CAINES, JEANETTE. *Daddy*. New York: Harper & Row, 1977.

CLIFTON, LUCILLE. *The Lucky Stone*. New York: Delacorte, 1979.

DR. SEUSS. *Are You My Mother?* New York: Random House, 1960.

EICHLER, M. *Martin's Father*. Chapel Hill, N.C.: Lollipop Power, 1977.

ELWIN, R. & PAULSE, M. *Asha's Mums*. Toronto: Women's Press, 1990.

FEELING, MURIEL. *Jambo Means Hello*. New York: Dial, 1974.

—   *Zamani Goes To Market*. New York: Seabury Press, 1970.

FRIEDMAN, INA R. *How My Parents Learned To Eat*. Boston: Houghton Mifflin, 1984.

GREENFIELD, ELOISE. *Talk About A Family*. New York: Lippincott, 1978.

NEWMAN, L. *Belinda's Bouquet*. Boston: Alyson Press, 1991.

ROBLES, AL. *Looking for Ifugao Mountain*. San Francisco: Children's Book Press, 1977.

SAN SOUCI, ROBERT D. AND STEPHEN T. JOHNSON. *The Samurai's Daughter*. New York: Dial, 1992.

SENFOZO, MARY. *Welcome Roberto! Bienvenido Roberto!* Chicago: Follett, 1969.

SIMON, NORMA. *All Kinds of Families*. Neil, IL.: Whitman Albert & Co., 1976.

SULLIVAN, CHARLES. *Children of Promise*. New York: Harry N. Abrams, Inc., 1991.

SURAT, MICHELLE MARIA. *Angel Child, Dragon Child*. New York: Scholastic, 1983.

TAX, MEREDITH. *Families*. Boston, MA: Little Brown & Co., 1981.

WILLHOITE, M. *Uncle What-Is-It Is Coming To Visit*. Boston: Alyson Press, 1993.

CHAPTER FOUR

Sharing and Support

Celebrating Connections

> ***I*** *always wanted to be somebody. If I make it, it's half because I was game enough to take a lot of punishment along the way and half because there were a lot of people who cared enough to help me.*
>
> —Althea Gibson

Introduction

This chapter is about making and keeping friends. It helps students define what makes a good friend and gives them the tools to be good friends themselves. The intent is for young people to base their friendships on qualities such as caring, supportive and fun, rather than by race, creed or color.

These positive qualities then become the basis for establishing and maintaining a peaceful and productive learning environment. Students are taught to appreciate the importance of making and keeping agreements, and how to behave in a disciplined manner during class meetings.

24

That's What Friends Are For

> *There are deep sorrows and killing cares in life, but the encouragement and love of friends were given us to make all difficulties bearable.*
>
> —John Oliver Hobbes

Purpose

Knowledge of oneself occurs in a social context. Someone who is totally isolated would not receive the feedback necessary to make the important distinctions that expand one's sense of self. To identify oneself as tall or short, light or dark, serious or jovial, requires the presence of others with whom to compare and contrast.

Acceptance by others — a sense of belonging — is essential to healthy self-esteem.

Many adults — fearing the unknown — tend to associate with others who are similar to themselves in terms of nationality, religion, economic class, and so forth. This "birds of a feather" syndrome may serve to maintain one's personal comfort level, but it also robs us of the opportunity to experience the cultural richness that diversity provides.

This activity is meant to help our children appreciate what attributes are important in friends so that they can be good friends themselves and select friends based upon true values rather than surface similarities.

Materials

One copy of Friends Are For Worksheet per student (reproduced on cardboard if possible)

Index Cards or Post-it® Notes, twelve per student

Procedure

1. Give each student a copy of the Friends Are For Worksheet and twelve index cards or Post-it® Notes.

2. Engage the students in a discussion of friendship and have them brainstorm what they like in a friend. Record these qualities on the board for all the students to see.

    You may want to add some of your own if you feel that the student –generated list needs to be expanded. Avoid setting up a situation where the students feel your answers are better than theirs.

    To increase students' awareness of cultural stereotypes and peer pressure, you can add items that raise such issues as: "same sneakers as mine," "same hair style as mine," "same skin color as mine," "same religion as mine," and so forth.

3. Now, instruct the students to pick the top six qualities that they feel are important in a good friend. Have them write one quality on each card.

4. Next, tell them to place the cards in order on their worksheet; the quality in space one being the most important, and so forth.

5. When they are finished placing all six cards in the appropriate spaces, ask for their attention. In order to check if, in fact, the most important qualities have been selected, propose the following scenario:

    Imagine that from all your friends you had to choose one to join you and your family on a cross-country car trip. Since you will be in a car most of the time, the friend you pick will be the person with whom you will spend all your time.

    Are there any other qualities you would want this person to have that we did not already mention?

6. Put on the board any additional thoughts the students have.

7. Invite them to consider if these newly identified qualities are more important than the six they already put on their chart. If so, they should rearrange their cards to accommodate these.

8. Here is another scenario to consider:

    Some of you may have heard of the disease, alopecia areata, that causes all of your hair to fall out. Bob Samuelson, one of the athletes in the

1992 Summer Olympics had it and all of his teammates shaved their heads in support of him.

What if you discovered that you had this disease? How might it change your life and what types of friends would you want to have around you?

9. Once again, add any other words to the list on the board, and have the students make any changes in their charts. They should now have a fairly clear sense of what matters to them in terms of friendship.

10. Ask the students to get into small groups of five or six and share with each other the qualities they selected as most important in friends.

11. Bring the students together and read with them, *That's What Friends Are For* by Carol Adorjan (New York: Scholastic Inc., 1990)

Friends Are For Worksheet

①

②

③

④

⑤

⑥

25

What Kind of Friend Am I?

> *You can hardly make a friend in a year, but you can lose one in an hour.*
>
> —Chinese Proverb

Purpose

The activity is a follow-up to the previous one. It supports students in developing the skills necessary to be a good friend.

Materials

Charts and cards from Activity 24, "That's What Friends Are For"

Procedure

Review with your students the lessons learned during the previous lesson on friendship.

1.   Distribute copies of the What Kind of Friend Am I? Worksheet, and help students fill it out as follows:

> *Start with the quality you identified as being the most important one for a good friend to have and write this on the top of the page.*
>
> *Now, list as many ways you can think of as to how someone shows that they have this quality. For example, if the quality is kindness, then friends show kindness by sharing things with you, saying nice things about you, inviting you to do things with them, listening to your problems, and so forth.*

Finally, think about how good a friend you are. To what extent do you have this quality? How often do you do the Acts of Friendship *you identified?*

Pick at least one thing you can do more often to be a better friend and write it on the Promise line.

Sign the page to show that you mean it.

2.   Invite the students to get into small groups and share their answers.

3.   During the course of the next few days, find opportunities to reinforce this lesson. Ask students to review their worksheets and report on progress.

4.   You may repeat this exercise in a week or two using the second and third highest friendship qualities that the students selected.

Alternate Version Procedure

1.   Review with your students the lessons learned during the previous lesson on friendship.

2.   Ask each student to say aloud what he/she selected as the most important quality of a friend and put these on the chalkboard or butcher paper.

3.   Identify the six most frequently mentioned qualities of a friend and underline them.

4.   Divide the class into six groups and have them each take one of the most frequently mentioned qualities of friends. Ask them to list as many ways they can think of for how someone shows that they have this quality. The same What Kind of Friend Am I? Worksheet can be used to record the group's answers.

5.   Next, have one student from each of these groups form a new group. Ask each expert to share with their new teammates the *Acts of Friendship* that their group identified.

6.   Focus on one of these themes each day for the next week or so.

  •   Discuss the Acts of Friendship each morning and ask the students to make promises as to which of these they will practice today.

  •   Throughout the day—after recess, after lunch, and so forth — check in with the students to see how well they're doing.

- At the end of the day—or at some other appropriate time—read a story to the students that has a character who models some of the friendship characteristics they identified. Have the students discuss the story, talking about what they liked about the character and so forth.

What Kind Of Friend Am I? Worksheet

FRIENDSHIP QUALITY

_____

ACTS OF FRIENDSHIP

_____

_____

_____

_____

_____

I PROMISE TO

_____

_____

_____

_____

_____

_____

_____

Name

26

Buddy Teams

> **Y**es'm, old friends is always best, 'less you can catch a new one that's fit to make an old one out of.
>
> —Sarah Orne Jewett

Purpose

Students will choose partners to support them in becoming the best students and persons they can be.

Procedure

1. Hold a class discussion on what a true friend does as opposed to what a false friend does. Introduce the theme by saying:

   Have you ever picked friends that didn't stand by you when you needed them? Or, have you ever felt bad because your friend got in trouble and you didn't because you didn't get caught? Have you ever wondered why some people have a lot of friends and some people hardly have any? Or maybe you wondered why today some people are good friends, but last week they weren't talking to each other. Today, we are going to choose a good friend or buddy, and this week we will see the results of what true friends we all can be.

2. Write on the chalkboard:

   TRUE FRIEND   FALSE FRIEND

3. Now say:

   Tell me some things that a true friend will do for you. Ask the students to tell you some things that a true friend would do, and record their responses on the chalkboard.

4.   Read the following examples to the class. After each one, discuss what a good friend would do, and record the responses.

    a.   *Cheryl and Marsha are buddies. They are going to have a big spelling test on Friday. Today is Wednesday and Cheryl knows all the words. Marsha hardly knows any words and even though she tries, she usually gets an F on her spelling tests. Think of several ways Cheryl can help Marsha. If Cheryl lets Marsha copy during the spelling test instead of helping Marsha learn the words, is that really helping Marsha?*

    b.   *Your best friend is having a big fight after school with the biggest bully in the fifth grade. You heard that the big bully is bringing five of his friends with him. Think of three different things you could do to help. What would eventually happen if you brought ten of your friends to back up your best friend?*

    c.   *You are playing kickball at recess with your class. Your buddy is on the opposite team. Your team is up. Your team is behind, but catching up, with the score of 7 to 8. Your teammate kicks the ball to the outfield and starts running. Your buddy goes to the outfield and starts running. Your buddy goes to catch the ball and runs into two other players. Your teammate is on second base running to third base. Everyone is cheering for him to run to home plate. Your buddy is on the ground, hurt, and doesn't get up. Think of four things you could immediately do.*

5.   Continue:

Now we are going to pick buddies—someone you will depend on, trust, and work well with. Do not pick your best friend or someone you know very well. Pick someone who you would like to get to know better. Someone who has a skill or talent you admire. Remember, we all have gifts to give to each other. Now, look across the room at the person you want for a partner.

Be sure students follow directions.

6.   Have students choose their buddies until everyone is paired up. If there is an uneven number of students, one buddy team may have three students.

7.   Each buddy team stands up and tells the class why they picked each other and what they can give to each other. Example:

I picked José because he's going to teach me my multiplication tables, and I'm going to help him to be a better kicker in kickball.

8. At the end of the week, have students tell the class what gifts they got from each other and what they learned from each other. They can also write each other thank-you notes.

Follow-Up Activities:

1. Have students pick for a buddy a person that they are uncomfortable with. The goal would be for them to be comfortable together and to learn about each other.

2. Have buddies sit together (share desks) and be responsible to each other for making sure all homework and class assignments are completed and turned in. Buddies could also do a joint project or report.

27

Promises to Keep

Seeing's believing, but feeling is God's own truth.

—Irish Proverb

Purpose

The purpose of this activity is to develop a classroom community based upon shared values regarding friendship and respect.

Procedure

1. Prepare yourself or have student groups prepare a chart of the *Friendship Qualities* and *Acts of Friendship* developed in the previous activity.

2. Review the lists with the class to decide which of the items could relate to the class as a whole.

    For example, if the *Friendship Quality* is "kindness" and a related *Act of Friendship* is "listening," then the class application could be "listen when someone else is speaking."

3. If the *Acts of Friendship* as written do not cover all of the important aspects of a safe and supportive classroom environment, you may want to do some coaching, asking questions such as:

    What would need to happen in the classroom so everyone feels supported and included?

    What would need to happen in the classroom so everyone can hear directions?

What agreement would we need to make in order for us to start class together so that no one misses anything and others aren't kept waiting for students who aren't here?

4.   Encourage students to say what they think. Accept their comments without evaluation and use their wording as much as possible.

5.   When all the classroom related *Acts of Friendship* have been identified, work with the students to eliminate duplications, combine similar items and reduce the total number to a length that is manageable. Seven items is probably as many as can be remembered.

6.   Discuss with the students the idea of making an agreement or a promise. Ask them if they would be willing to promise to keep these agreements in order to have the classroom be safe and workable for everyone.

7.   Write the final list of Classroom Agreements on a large poster for all the students to sign, or on individual sheets such as the Classroom Agreements Worksheet.

You may want to send a copy home to the students' parents and guardians to inform them of their children's agreements. Having parents sign and return them is a way of ensuring that they got the information.

SAMPLE AGREEMENTS

- Listen when someone else is speaking

- Be on time

- Be prepared

- Follow instructions

- Be nice to myself and to each other

- Work to the best of my ability

- Confidentiality (What is shared in the classroom stays in the classroom.)

COMMON CHALLENGES

When a student does not follow an agreement, ask the student if he or she is aware of breaking an agreement, and if so, which one. The student usually knows. Once he or she acknowledges the broken agreement, ask if he or she is willing to recommit to keeping the promise. If the student says yes, restate his or her promise and acknowledge him or her for being willing to be responsible for keeping his or her word.

If the student says no, discuss the issue until you and he or she reach a new agreement. The key here is not to make the breaking of the guideline an issue that requires punitive action. Be firm and clear, but not confrontational. When the guidelines are self-enforced, there is a much higher level of cooperation from all students.

Peer coaching may be used to support students in keeping their agreements. Class meetings — described in the next activity — are a good place to discuss Classroom Agreements.

Classroom Agreements Worksheet

The following list of **Classroom Agreements** were identified by our class.

_____

_____

_____

_____

_____

_____

I know what these agreements mean and promise to keep them.

_____   _____
Student Signature   Date

28

My Circle of Friends

> *The world is round and the place which may seem like the end may also be only the beginning.*
>
> —Ivy Baker Priest

Purpose

This activity is intended to help you establish a regular routine of class meetings or sharing sessions that can be used on an on-going basis to deepen student's sense of belonging, as well as to deal with specific issues that arise in most classrooms.

During this structured time, students will learn to:

- Share their feelings in a responsible manner

- Listen to others with greater patience and compassion

- Appreciate that they are not alone in dealing with difficult situations

- Cope with problems in more effective ways by hearing how others have resolved similar issues.

As their teacher, you will increase your understanding of your students and their thoughts, feelings, desires, fears and challenges which will better prepare you to help them academically and socially.

Procedure

1.   Brainstorm with your students objects or gestures that connote friendship in different cultures. Some example follow:

Objects	*Gestures*
• friendship ring	• handshake
• yellow rose	• high five
• lei (Hawaiian)	• American Sign Language (ASL) gesture for "I Love You"
• peace pipe/talking stick (Native American)	
• teddy bear	• peace sign
	• bowing (Japanese)
	• "Namasté" (Hindu)

2.   Use one of these objects or gestures as a way of focusing the students. Bring the students into a full circle so that everyone can see everyone else. Whoever is holding the object is the center of attention. It is this person's turn to share, everyone else listens.

The object is passed around the circle until everyone has had a chance to speak.

Students are always welcome to "pass" if they have nothing to say at this time.

3.   Remind students of the classroom agreements, especially those that are relevant to this activity.

It is, of course, strongly desirable that all members of the class physically participate in the circle. In rare instances, however, when an individual student is unwilling to commit to keeping the agreements during Circle Time, you may have him or her sit outside the circle. Give an assignment that can be done quietly at a desk. The task might be related to the topic that is being discussed by the students in the circle. For example, a topic for Circle Time could be, "Share about a time you did something nice for someone," which could also be a theme for an essay or drawing that a student could work on outside of the circle. A student outside the circle can choose to join the group by recommitting to the class agreements.

4.   It is recommended that you do a Circle of Friends on a frequent basis — perhaps daily, at least once per week. The length of activity depends upon how much time is available, as well as the age and maturity of your students and the level of interest in the particular topic.

If time runs out before every student has had a chance to share, pick up where you left off next time. You could also put a time limit on each student's sharing. For example, each student says just one word to describe how he or she feels this morning, or each student gets one minute to share.

Circle time may also be done in small groups rather than as a full class. The next activity will provide guidelines for how to set up these student support groups.

5.   Circle of Friends may be used to address particular issues such as:

   • classroom agreements
   • feelings related to an upcoming test
   • an incident in the playground
   • excessive teasing of a particular student or group
   • planning a field trip
   • loss of a major athletic event
   • social, political or community issue that is getting a lot of attention
   • loss of a pet
   • death of a school mate.

6.   Circle time can also be a regularly scheduled part of the classroom program. For example:

   • in the morning, to focus the students on plans for the day
   • after lunch, to refocus for the afternoon
   • at the end of the day, to review and bring closure to the day's events
   • as a part of certain subjects to discuss feelings about a story, film or lesson.

7.   Possible topics for Circle of Friends—clustered around the themes of this book—include:

   • Identity
       —something I like about myself_____
       —something I like about being _____
           (African American, Hispanic, Jewish, Native American, Vietnamese, and so forth)
       —something that makes me special.

- Belonging
  - —things I do to be a good friend
  - —what I like about my friends
  - —a time when I was new and didn't know how to meet friends
  - —a time someone helped me feel like I belonged
  - —a time when I trusted someone and they came through
  - —a time when I trusted someone and they let me down.

- Achievement
  - —a goal I achieved recently
  - —something I intend to achieve this year
  - —a successful person I admire
  - —the best school-related achievement I ever got and how I earned it
  - —other areas of my life where I feel successful (sports, musical talent, friends, at home, and so forth).

29

Everyone Belongs

> *I*t *really boils down to this: that all life is interrelated. We are all caught in an inescapable network of mutuality, tied into a single garment of destiny. Whatever affects one directly, affects all indirectly.*
>
> —Martin Luther King, Jr.

Purpose

In this activity, students will appreciate that everyone belongs, everyone is needed and has a contribution to make. Students will also recognize the importance of working together as a team to accomplish a common goal. They will become aware of the relationship between personal success and group or team success, and will realize that by shifting from personal self-interest to concern for the needs of others, their own needs get taken care of in the process.

Note: In advance, prepare sets of broken square puzzles as diagrammed.

Procedure

1. Divide the class into groups of five students. (If there are extra students, have these students function as "observers." The observer's job is to watch the process, notice how the team approaches putting together the puzzle, and be prepared to report during the debriefing.)

2. Tell them:

    The purpose of this activity is for you to experience the interrelationship of everyone and the connection between personal success and group success. The goal of this activity is for each of you to put together a square that is equal in size to the square of everyone else on your team.

The operating instructions are as follows:

- *Players may not talk, point, or in any way communicate with the other people in the group.*
- *Players may give pieces to other participants, but may not just take pieces from another person.*
- *Players may not throw their pieces into the center for others to take; they must give the pieces directly to an individual.*
- *Players may give away pieces to their puzzle, even after they have already formed a square.*

In order for the game to work, each player must make a commitment to the purpose, goal, and operating instructions. Is there anyone not willing to follow the operating instructions?

(Answer questions or concerns. If there are still some unwilling to participate, assign these students as observers.)

Those of you who are observers are to watch the process, notice how the team approaches putting the puzzles together, and be prepared to report back to us.

3. Allow enough time for each group to complete the activity. Ask groups who are finished to wait quietly until the others are done. You might let the students who are finished talk among themselves about their experience of the activity.

You might also ask them to give clues to the groups who are still working on the puzzle, without revealing too much and spoiling the fun of discovery.

4. Bring the class together to debrief:

What worked?
What got in the way of success?
Based on this experience, what would you say is important for individual success and group success?

(Responses to the last question can be written on the board, under the heading "Guidelines for Individual and Group Success.")

5. You may want to make the following concluding remarks:

This exercise serves as a model for how we can create a classroom, school, and society where everybody wins. Recognizing that there is no scarcity, there are no missing pieces, we realize that the universe already has everything that any of us could need or want. We each have a contribution to make to the whole. We can each look at what other people need and give what we have to give. We can be open to what other people have contributed to us. Then, like magic, it all comes together. What is needed is a commitment to our own personal success and also a commitment to contribute to the success of everyone else in the class.

Supplementary Activity

A nice way to end this activity is to read *Horton Hears A Who* to the class. This delightful book stresses this same theme—that everyone's contribution is important, that we are all indispensable pieces to the overall puzzle. (Dr. Seuss, *Horton Hears a Who:* New York: Random House, 1954.)

Everyone Belongs Puzzle Pieces

To make the puzzle pieces for this activity, use poster board or heavy coated paper. For each group of five or six students, cut five 6-inch squares. Using the following patterns, cut each of the squares into pieces. (Note: all the A's are the same size.)

Now, in order to mix the pieces up, put them in envelopes as follows:

Envelope A: pieces I, H, E   Envelope B: pieces A, A, A, C
Envelope C: pieces A, J   Envelope D: pieces D, F
Envelope E: pieces G, B, F, C

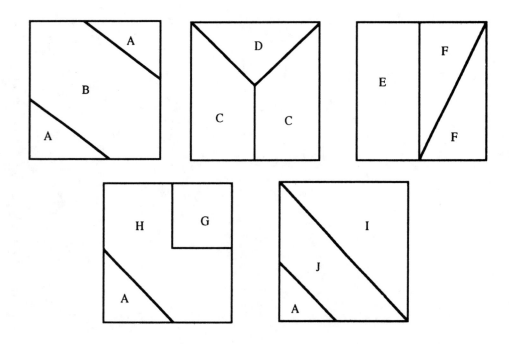

30

Giver's Gain

> *E*ach friend represents a world in us, a world possibly not born until they arrive, and it is only by this meeting that a new world is born.
>
> —Anais Nin

Purpose

Students will learn that what they give to others, is what comes back to them (giver's gain).

Procedure

1. Ask the students to name someone who is very well-liked at school. It can be a teacher, aide, any adult or student who is a positive and good person. Pick one of the responses.

2. Now explore with the class why this person is so popular.

3. Cluster student responses around common traits such as: friendly, talented, smart, attractive, and so forth.

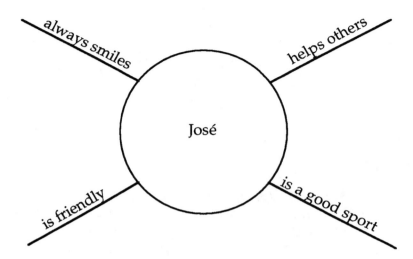

4.   Ask the class:

What does José do or give to you that makes you like him? Be specific.

Chart responses on the board.

Examples:
— He got the nurse when I fell.
— He loaned me a quarter when I lost my lunch money.
— He showed me how to solve the math problem.

5.   Ask students:

Would you like to be more well-liked? What can you do to become more popular and attract more friends?

Have children turn to a partner and tell three things that they could do themselves to attract more friends. (Be sure to tell them they must be positive things.)

6.   Next say:

You may have heard the expression, "What goes around, comes around." This means that if you are a good person who is kind and friendly, you are more likely to attract friends who are good to you in return. On the other hand, if you are unkind and unfriendly, you are likely to find it difficult to make friends and keep them.

You may also have heard, "Do unto others as you would have them do unto you." We are calling this "Giver's Gain" — what you put out, you will get back.

Here are a few more examples:
— *If you show anger towards others, you are likely to trigger their anger back at you.*
— *If you are friendly to others, others are more likely to respond in a friendly manner.*
— *If you are helpful and kind to others, others will be helpful and kind to you.*
— *If you are honest and truthful in your dealings with others, people are more apt to be truthful with you.*
— *If you are stingy and mean to others, others are not likely to be generous with you.*

7. At the end of each day, let students acknowledge others who they saw giving in a positive way.

Follow-Up Activity:

1. Student assignment will be to practice "Giver's Gain" and write a paragraph describing what they did and what happened.

31

WHAM (What's Hot About Me)

Most people die with their music still locked up inside them.

—Benjamin Disraeli

Purpose

Students will recognize 15 great characteristics about themselves.

Materials

Pencils
Paper

Procedure

1.   Start the lesson saying:

     Today we are going to discover many wonderful things about us. Some of these qualities we probably already know, some we aren't sure of, and some qualities will surprise us. Deep down inside, we have many great qualities that are waiting to come out. We are going to get into small groups and make a WHAM List: a list of "What's Hot About Me!"

2.   Divide class into small groups of three or four. Let students pick their own groups and encourage them to be with their friends.

3.   Give students paper and pencil and ask them to write their names on the paper.

4.   Now, tell them:

> *All students in one group will help one person at a time list 15 of their great qualities.*

5.   Demonstrate the exercise by picking a student from the class and writing his or her name on the board. Say:

> *Give me five good qualities about this person.*

(Encourage class to answer spontaneously and quickly. Write each response on the board.)

Example: <u>Lisa</u>

1. fast runner

2. good in math

3. honest

4. kind

5. friendly

6.   As soon as each list is completed, go to the next person in the group.

7.   After all lists are completed, ask students:

> *What did you learn about yourself?*
> *What did you learn about someone else in your group?*

8.   Make sure that the lists contain the name of the person along with their qualities.

9.   Have students rewrite their own WHAM lists, checking for spelling and neat handwriting.

Collect and compile lists into a class book for all to read.

Note: *You may choose to shorten or lengthen the list of great characteristics if you anticipate any problems or to suit your class. As you repeat this activity, it will become easier and show the progress your students are making.*

Follow-Up Activities

1. Encourage students to make their own WHAM lists periodically. If they add "I am" in front of each word, the lists become affirmations and can be used to increase self-esteem.

2. Teachers should make WHAM lists to set an example.

3. Make a bulletin board of students' lists.

３２

Put Ups

> *If the only prayer you say in your entire life is "Thank you," that would suffice.*
>
> —Meister Eckhart

Purpose

Students will be able to recognize positive traits in themselves and others and develop a habit of talking about positive traits.

Procedure

1. Discuss the concept of a positive or negative atmosphere in the classroom, and how it affects us.

    For example:

    A negative atmosphere is created when students and teachers use put-downs, pointing out only negative things about each other. A positive atmosphere is created when we look for and talk about the good points. We are going to practice 'put-ups' to help create a more positive atmosphere.

2. Use this daily exercise for 10 to 15 minutes for a week or more.

3. Seat students in a circle facing each other.

4. Explain "Sharing Circle" rules as follows:

    — Students take turns, going around the circle until everyone has spoken. One person speaks at a time.
    — No interruptions, laughing at, or comments allowed.
    — Listen to the person who is speaking.

— When it is your turn, share one brief answer on the topic given.

5.   Write the topic on the chalkboard, say it out loud, then allow a minute or more for children to think before beginning the circle.

Day 1 Topic:
"Something that I like in other people is . . . "
   Suggested examples you can give before starting: "I like people who are honest. I like people who listen to me."

Day 2 Topic:
"Something I like in myself is . . . "
   Examples: "I like that I'm smart. I can keep a secret."

Day 3 Topic:
"Something I like or appreciate about the person to my right is . . . "
   Examples: "She is funny. He is friendly. He draws pictures for me." You need to emphasize that even in someone you dislike, there are qualities you can appreciate.

Day 4 Topic:
"A time I was praised for something was the time . . . "
   Example: "My friend said I was a good pitcher in baseball."

Day 5 Topic:
"A time I pleased someone else was the time . . . "

Day 6 Topic:
"When I felt bad and someone made me feel better was the time that . . . "

Note: *This activity can also be done in smaller groups if the class is uncomfortable.*

Follow-Up Activities

1.   Take two jars and some beans, marbles, or other objects. Each time you hear a put-down, place a bean in the "down jar." Each time you hear a put-up, place a bean in the "up jar." The object is to see how long it takes for the "up jar" to be full.

2.   Do bulletin board of put-ups. Students can write put-ups for their classmates.

3.   Encourage journal writing on any of the topics above.

4.   Send a worksheet home to parents asking them to list qualities they like about their child.

Part II—Key Learnings

O—🔑   Everyone is unique.

O—🔑   I know how to make and keep good friends.

O—🔑   Everyone belongs here.

O—🔑   What makes a good friend is the same in all cultures.

O—🔑   We are all part of a family.

O—🔑   I am friends with all kinds of different people.

O—🔑   Families, like people, are unique.

O—🔑   Having friends from different cultures makes my life more interesting.

O—🔑   All cultures are special.

O—🔑   By being a good friend, I will have good friends.

Part II—Teacher Checklist
Getting to Know My Students and Their Families

❑ Have I taken the time to get to know my students as individuals — their likes and dislikes, fears and dreams?

❑ Have I identified each student's strengths and given each of them opportunities to experience being successful?

❑ Am I helping my students to develop healthy relationships with their classmates, supporting them in solving their own problems and encouraging them to appreciate family and cultural diversity?

❑ How well do I know my students' families and have my efforts to reach out to them been effective?

❑ Have I found ways of facilitating communication with families whose native language is different from mine?

❑ Have I informed my students' parents and guardians about our educational objectives and how they can help at home?

❑ How many families and community members representing all cultures and family structures have been in my classroom to interact with the students?

❑ Have I discovered that prejudice among students often reflects biases that they learn from their families, and have I formulated a plan for educating parents and guardians on the value of diversity?

❑ Have I recognized approaches to parenting that do not enhance children's self-esteem, and have I formulated a plan for educating parents on the importance of self-esteem and how it is developed?

Chapter Four   *Suggested Student Readings*

ADLER, C.S. *Always and Forever Friends*. New York: Ticknor and Fields, 1988.

ADOFF, ARNOLD. *All the Colors of the Race*. New York: Lothrop, 1982.

ADORJAN, CAROL. *That's What Friends Are For*. New York: Scholastic Inc., 1990.

BANG, MOLLY. *The Paper Crane*. New York: Greenwillow Books, 1985.

BELPRÈ PURA. *The Rainbow-Colored Horse*. New York: Frederick Warner, 1978.

CHIN, STEVEN A. *When Justice Failed: The Fred Koremastsu Story*. Austin, TX: Steck-Vaughn Co., 1993.

DR. SEUSS. *Horton Hears a Who*. New York: Random House, 1954.

ISADORA, RACHEL. *Friends*. New York: Greenwillow, 1990.

JAKATA STORIES. *The Value of Friends*. Oakland, CA: Dharma Press, 1990.

PERETZ, I. L. *The Seven Good Years*. Philadelphia: The Jewish Publication Society of America, 1984.

TAYLOR, MILDRED D. *Let the Circle Be Unbroken*. New York: Dial, 1981.

ZOLOTOW, CHARLOTTE. *The Storm Book*. New York: HarperCollins, 1989.

PART III

RESPECT
AND
PERSONAL RESPONSIBILITY

Making Life Work

*Life is what we make it,
always has been,
always will be.*

— Grandma Moses

	Experience (Internal)	Express (External)
Others	Interdependence	Social Responsibility
Self	Independence	Personal Responsibility

CHAPTER FIVE

Empowerment

The Force Be With You

Mama exhorted her children at every opportunity to "jump at de sun." We might not land on the sun, but at least we would get off the ground.

—Zora Neal Hurston

Introduction

The activities in this chapter are meant to empower students to be responsible for their own experience of self-worth, so that they are able to maintain their self-esteem even in the face of obstacles such as racial prejudice and stereotypes. The intent here is not to minimize the adverse affects of bigotry, racism, sexism and homophobia. Quite the contrary, we believe it is absolutely essential that schools not tolerate intolerance.

However, until we succeed in eradicating ignorance in the world, we can at least teach our children some tools for not internalizing the negative messages that may be directed at them.

33

Ain't It Awful

---

*T*he things which hurt, instruct.

—Benjamin Franklin

---

*C*haracter cannot be developed in ease and quiet. Only through experience of trial and suffering can the soul be strengthened, vision cleared, ambition inspired, and success achieved.

—Helen Keller

Purpose

The purpose of this activity is to empower students by encouraging them to be responsible for how they experience situations in life. The activities in this chapter work most effectively as a complete unit, with each exercise following in sequence.

Procedure

1.   Introduce the activity by making remarks similar to these:

   Have you ever thought that it's really crummy being a kid? That adults get to do all the good stuff, while they order kids around and make them do things they themselves don't want to do?

   Have you ever wished you had a magic button you could push to go directly to age 18 or 21 without all the hassles of growing up?

Have you ever had the feeling that adults just don't understand what kids have to put up with these days?

If so, you're going to have the chance now to get all your complaints off your chest, once and for all. If you feel that your gripes haven't been heard up to now, today's your day!

2. Have the students put their chairs into a semicircle. Brainstorm with your class the question "What's so awful about being a kid?" Write the list on the chalkboard.

3. After the brainstorm, read them the story *Alexander and the Terrible, Horrible, No Good, Very Bad Day*, by Judith Viorst (New York: Antheneum Press, 1972).

4. Review with your students the list of "awful things" the class brainstormed, and have them copy the ones they think are the worst, somewhere between five and ten items from the list.

5. Then, have them pick out the very worst things about being a kid, from their viewpoint, and draw a picture or write a story about their own terrible, horrible, no good, very bad days.

6. Proceed to the next activity, Maybe Yes Maybe No.

34

Maybe Yes, Maybe No

---

*P*rovidence has hidden a charm in difficult undertakings which is appreciated only by those who dare to grapple with them.

—Anne-Sophie Swetchine

---

*N*othing is good or bad, but thinking makes it so.

—William Shakespeare
Hamlet

Purpose

The meaning of life's events lies in our perception or interpretation of them. You may have noticed that different people often have very different interpretations of the same event.

Have you also realized that you sometimes change your own mind about an event after you get more information?

Through this activity, students get to see that there is power in accepting things as they are, in deferring judgment about whether something is good or bad until we see how things turn out.

Procedure

1.   Read the following old Chinese Taoist story of "The Man and the Horse" to your class.

> *A very old Chinese Taoist story describes a farmer in a poor country village. He was considered very well-to-do, because he owned a horse which he used for plowing and for transportation. One day his horse ran away. All his neighbors exclaimed how terrible this was, but the farmer simply said, "Maybe yes, maybe no."*
>
> *A few days later the horse returned and brought two wild horses with it. The neighbors all rejoiced at his good fortune, but the farmer just said, "Maybe yes, maybe no."*
>
> *The next day the farmer's son tried to ride one of the wild horses; the horse threw him and broke his leg. The neighbors all offered their sympathy for his misfortune, but the farmer again said, "Maybe yes, maybe no."*
>
> *The next week conscription officers came to the village to take young men for the army. They rejected the farmer's son because of his broken leg. When the neighbors told him how lucky he was the farmer replied, "Maybe yes, maybe no."*

2.   Refer back to the list of awful things about being a kid that students wrote for the previous activity. Ask them to consider the possibility that the "awful" events could be looked at from a different viewpoint that would make them appear to be blessings in disguise.

3.   Have them select one event from the list and write a brief paragraph explaining what happened, why they thought it was awful, and how they could "reframe" the event to see it as a lucky thing.

4.   Next, invite them to look back at the picture they drew of the worst thing about being a kid.

5.   Have them pretend that they are looking back on it from several months or years into the future when enough other things have happened so that they can appreciate how that "worst thing" was actually a necessary step in their lives. Ask them to write a paragraph or two explaining how the "worst thing" they are dealing with today brought them some good luck, taught them a valuable lesson, or turned out not to be so bad after all. (For example, one girl had felt that the worst thing for her was her best friend was moving away to another town. She then saw this as an

opportunity to become more outgoing so that she could make new friends).

6. Divide the class into small groups to discuss their stories.

7. Bring the class together again as a full group, and complete the activity with a discussion. Possible discussion questions:

> *Did your reinterpretation of the 'worst thing' agree with those suggested by other members of your group?*
>
> *Are you beginning to see the situation as not so bad as you first thought? If yes, explain what you now believe to be true about your 'most awful thing.' If no, what would have to happen in order for you to see this situation as less awful?*
>
> *Consider the situations identified by others as the most awful things about their lives right now. Did they seem that awful to you? Why or why not?*
>
> *Is it easier to reframe someone else's event than your own?*
>
> *Does it help to know that other people also have 'worst things' in their lives? Give examples from today's activity to explain your answers.*

35

$E + R = O$

> Experience is not what happens to a man; it is what a man does with what happens to him.
>
> —Aldous Huxley

Purpose

The next couple of activities work together to demonstrate the concept that we are responsible for our own feelings, to introduce the idea that other people don't "make us" feel things, and to demonstrate that we have control over how we feel and how we react to others.* They are most effective when done as a unit since the students are not asked to interact with the concepts until after the third part, and such interaction is essential to integrating the information into meaningful lessons.

People often fall into the trap of blaming other people for how they feel and for what happens to them, then they end up looking for solutions to their problems by focusing on changing supposed outside causes. It is much more effective, however, to look inside ourselves: regardless of who is to blame, we are at least in charge of how we feel. Taking the point of view that we are responsible for our responses to the outside events gives us more power.

Procedure

1. Write the formula E + R = O on the chalkboard. Then explain the following to the students:

---

* The next two activities are adapted with permission from Jack Canfield. They appear in *101 Ways to Develop Student Self–Esteem and Responsibility* by Jack Canfield and Frank Siccone, Needham Heights, MA: Allyn and Bacon, 1995.

"**E** stands for all the 'events' of our lives.

"**R** stands for our 'response' to those events.

"**O** stands for the 'outcomes' we experience."

2.   Continue with the following remarks seeking ways to involve students, eliciting their comments so that it is more an interactive dialogue than a lecture.

What most people complain about in their lives are the "outcomes" of this equation. For instance, people complain about feeling hurt, feeling sad, feeling guilty, feeling angry, being yelled at by their parents, being lonely, getting failing grades in school, or how their friends treat them.

These are all "O's" that resulted from the responses (R's) used to deal with the events—the "E's"—that occurred.

For instance, would it be possible to come into this classroom where there are many, many people and end up feeling lonely? ("Yes.") Would it be possible to come into this same classroom and end up making a lot of friends? ("Yes.") It's the same classroom. The "E" is the same: there are the same people, in the same circumstances. Yet two people can enter the same room and produce two very different outcomes for themselves. How is this possible?

It happens because the "R," the "response," of the different individuals is different. For example, I might enter, look around the room, and decide that everyone is too strange, too weird, too unfamiliar, unfriendly, better than I am or different from me. I would then keep my distance and avoid contact with anyone. The "outcome" for me would be feeling lonely, thinking that the class was unfriendly and I end up not having had any fun.

Another person might come into the same room, at the same time, with the same circumstances and go up to someone and say, "Hi, my name is Sheila, and I just moved here from Cleveland. Who are you?" That person chose a different response to the same set of circumstances and events, the same "E," and as a result, she produced a different 'outcome' in her life.

Often what we do in life is to hope, pray, or demand that the "E," the outside event, change. We often hear this in the form of "If only's." "If only my teacher were more understanding. If only my father were more loving. If only my friend understood how I feel. If only . . ."

The fact is that the "E's"—those environmental influences and the other people in our lives—rarely do change in the way we want them to. It's not impossible, but it doesn't happen very often. In order to produce a different, more desirable outcome, we have to change our own behavior and our own responses.

If I want a different outcome in the classroom, I'm going to have to do something different: reach out, participate more, raise my hand, do my homework on time, or ask for more help from the teacher. If I want a different response from my mother, I'm going to have to do something different in order to get her to respond differently to me.

3. Next draw the numbers **2 + 2 = 4** on the board.

Now, 2 + 2 = 4 and will always equal 4 from now until the end of time. If you don't like the outcome 4, you will have to change either the first or the second 2. You've already seen that other people and outside events are not likely to change very quickly or easily. But you do have the power to change your response. You can change your 2 to a 3 or 4 or 5 or 6, producing a different result or "outcome."

Sometimes the events in your life have already happened. Your friend Shawna's family is going to move out of town. At that point you have a choice—you can choose to be sad by telling yourself that no one will ever like you again the same way Shawna did. You can tell yourself that you're going to be all alone, and then you'll feel lonely. A different response would be to say to yourself, "There are many people in the world with whom I can have a great friendship. I'll start to play with other kids and make new friends right away." This response produces a totally different outcome.

If you hit a baseball through a neighbor's window and start to imagine negative outcomes such as being grounded for a month, you're likely to feel nervous inside—that is the outcome you have produced by imagining a negative event in the future that hasn't happened yet. The baseball going through the window didn't produce that. Your thinking bad thoughts produced it. Another choice is to realize that you've make a mistake. You can own up to it, talk to the neighbor, and work to replace the window. Then you'll produce a good feeling inside of yourself. The event does not determine how you feel. What you say to yourself (auditory) and what pictures you choose to run in your head (visual) determine how you feel.

"E + R = O" means that if you want changes in your life, you need to stop blaming the events, circumstances, and other people for what happens to you and start focusing on your thoughts, internal images, and actions—your response. That's where your power is to produce the kinds of outcomes you truly want.

36

Sticks and Stones

Some things have to be believed to be seen.

—Ralph Hodgson

Purpose

Sticks and stones may break my bones, but names can really hurt me. This interactive demonstration makes the explanation about "E + R = O" even more real for students, and helps them not react or feel hurt when others call them names.

Procedure

1.   Say the following:

The "E + R = O" formula works well in terms of seeing how we let other people "make us feel bad." For example, suppose I go up to Mary and tell her, "Mary, you have green hair." Would that make you feel bad? (Mary would usually answer no. If she says yes, keep asking different students until someone says no.) "Why not?" "Because I know I don't have green hair." So it's not what I say to Mary that affects how she feels. What Mary believes to be true about her hair is what determines her emotional response to me.

Any time someone says something to you and you feel hurt, that's because at some level you have a doubt about yourself in that area. If I say, "You have green hair!" and you know you don't, there is no problem. The same is true with anything else in your life. If someone calls you stupid and you feel hurt by it, they didn't hurt your feelings. Your self-doubt about your own intelligence is what created the pain. (The way to get beyond this is to use affirmations, such as "I am an intelligent person. I am smart.")

2.   At this point conduct a discussion about things people have said that have hurt your students. Ask them to look inside to see if they have self-doubts about that particular issue in their lives.

By now, your classroom environment should be safe enough for students to feel comfortable talking about name calling, including racial slurs and homophobic remarks. You might ask, "What names have you been called that have negative connotations? What are they supposed to mean? What is hurtful or offensive to you about these words? How can we hear them without taking it personally or without being hurt or offended?"

3.   Point out that much of our self-image—including our self-doubts and hurts—is a function of early environmental factors such as parent and family admonitions, cultural and societal prejudices and so forth. By taking responsibility for ourselves we have the opportunity to get out from under these influences.

4.   Secondly, even though we now realize that each of us can experience being responsible for our own self-doubts and hurts, this does not give us permission to be insensitive and cruel to others, as in putting down and teasing others.

Note: *Among the most common taunts used by students even in the most socially-conscious communities are homophobic terms such as "queer" and "faggot." Remarks against gays and lesbians should be treated the same way you would respond to racial, ethnic or religious bigotry. Students should be educated to the fact that such name-calling is offensive, inappropriate and harmful to a segment of the student population.*

The negative consequences of societal homophobia are reflected in the following statistics:

- *One in five adolescent lesbians and 45 percent of adolescent gay males suffer assault or harassment due to sexual orientation according to a study conducted by the National Gay and Lesbian Task Force.*

- *Physical attacks have been experienced by 41 percent of gay youth as reported in the Journal of Interpersonal Violence (Hunter, Joyce. 1990, pp. 295-300).*

- *Gay males and lesbians are five times more likely than straight students to skip school out of fear for their safety concludes a survey of 4,000 students conducted by the Massachusetts Department of Education.*

- *Even more alarming, this same Massachusetts study discovered that nearly 37 percent of gay and lesbian high schoolers try to kill themselves each year. This is two to three times higher than heterosexual youth. The U.S. Department of Health and Human Services confirms that there are 500,000 attempted suicides annually which extrapolates to one lesbian/gay attempt every 35 minutes.*

- *In calculating the actual suicide rate, this same federal department found that 30 percent of all youth suicides (5,000 annually) are by lesbian/gay youth — which is the equivalent of one gay youth death every 5 hours and 45 minutes.*

For additional information and resources for combating anti-gay bias in schools, contact: The Gay, Lesbian and Straight Education Network (GLSEN), 121 West 27th Street, Suite 804, New York, NY 10001 or visit their Web page, http://www.glsen.org/.

3 7

Shattering Stereotypes·

---

*E*very bigot was once a child free of prejudice.

—Sister Mary De Lourdes

Purpose

To help students recognize and analyze the myths of stereotyping, become aware of forces which influence stereotyping, and learn to relate to people free from the limits of stereotypes.

Materials

Fact sheets A-B-C
Pencils

Procedure

1.   In a large group, explain the purpose of the activity and use Fact Sheets to introduce the topic of stereotypes (copy or use as a transparency).

2.   Divide the class into small discussion groups (6 - 8 members). Their support groups can be used for this purpose.

---

3.   Distribute the Shattering Stereotypes Worksheet and have the students complete them and then share their individual responses with their small group.

4.   Re-assemble as a large group and discuss:

What do you think stereotyping is?

What were the stereotypes discussed in your group?

Which stereotypes bother you the most?

How do we learn stereotypes?

What can we do to eliminate stereotyping?

How can we deal with people who tease us by using ethnic humor or slurs?

5.   You can remind students of the lessons learned in "E+R=O" and "Sticks and Stones."

Note: *The examples of stereotypes used on Fact Sheet A are taken from a survey conducted in 1994 by Louis Harris on behalf of the National Conference of Christians and Jews.*

The poll discovered that not only does bigotry exist among white Americans, but ethnic groups believe stereotypes about each other. For example, a majority of Asians believe Latinos tend to have more children than they can support. Latinos consider blacks are inclined toward crime and violence. African Americans, in turn, believe that Latinos lack the drive to succeed and that Asians are devious in business dealings.

The good news emerging from this study is that younger respondents were less likely than older respondents to hold negative stereotypes of other ethnic groups in every category.

FACT SHEET A

Definition of a stereotype:
to categorize a group based on some presupposed characteristics.

- Stereotypes may be negative and/or positive.

- Stereotypes are learned.

Examples:

- Muslims belong to a religion that condones or supports terrorism.

- Latinos tend to have bigger families than they are able to support.

- African Americans want to live on welfare.

- Jews, when it comes to choosing between people and money, will choose money.

- Asian Americans are unscrupulously crafty and devious in business.

- Whites are insensitive to other people and have a long history of bigotry and prejudice.

FACT SHEET B

What are some stereotyping techniques?

- Exaggeration or distortion of a physical feature or behavior

- Use of key words or phrases (words that over-generalize)

Examples:

- Use of loaded words (words that may create negative images)

Examples:

slobs	pigs
untrained	dangerous
welfare	poverty

FACT SHEET C

How we learn stereotypes:

- neighbors

- friends

- movies

- school books

- library books

- comic books

- family

- television

- cartoons

Shattering Stereotypes Worksheet

Directions: Complete each statement with the name of a group which you feel is most commonly stereotyped. Then put a T or F in the column to show whether you believe that this statement is True or False. Then in the last column write in the name of someone you know or know about who does not fit the stereotype.

		True or False	Name of someone who does not fit stereotype
1.	Most _____ wear feathers and live in teepees.	____	_____
2.	_____ are pretty but dumb.	____	_____
3.	Most _____ people are stingy.	____	_____
4.	Most _____ have fat wives and lots of children.	____	_____
5.	Most _____ families are on welfare.	____	_____
6.	_____ cannot be trusted.	____	_____
7.	_____ all look alike.	____	_____
8.	_____ really like to drink.	____	_____
9.	_____ usually hang around in street gangs.	____	_____
10.	_____ are stronger and smarter than _____.	____	_____
11.	_____ have good singing voices and dance well.	____	_____
12.	Most _____ own their own businesses.	____	_____
13.	_____ are not good at math.	____	_____
14.	_____ are rednecks who wear cowboy hats, drink beer and hate people who are different.	____	_____

This is the confession of a half–educated man. My education prepared me superbly for a bird's-eye view of the world; it taught me how to recognize easily and instantly the things that differentiate one place or one people from another. But my education failed to teach me that the principal significance of such differences is that they are largely without significance. My education failed to grasp the fact that beyond the differences are realities scarcely comprehended because of their shattering simplicity. And the simplest reality of all is that the human community is one—greater than any of its parts, greater than the separateness imposed by actions, greater than the divergent faiths and allegiances or the depth and color of varying cultures.

—Norman Cousins

38

Odd Jobs Scavenger Hunt

> *H*istorically our own culture has relied for the creation of rich and contrasting values upon many artificial distinctions, the most striking of which is sex ... if we are to achieve a richer culture, rich in contrasting values we must recognize the whole gambit of human possibilities, and so weave a less arbitrary social fabric, one in which each diverse human gift will find a fitting place.
>
> — Margaret Mead

Background

Gender-based stereotypes also need to be challenged. Since women have entered the workforce some progress has been made in gaining parity with men but much remains to be done. Women continue to earn less than men and the number of women in high-level executive positions remains small.

Research indicates a pattern of diminishing self-esteem as girls grow older. "Younger girls tend to be much more confident, reliant and straight forward," according to Annie G. Rogers, researcher associate at the Harvard Project on the Psychology of Women and the Development of Girls.

Among the many studies that have documented the phenomenon, a 1990 nationwide poll commissioned by the American Association of University Women revealed a dramatic drop in self-esteem among girls as they enter adolescence.

Using a basic self-esteem indicator to track positive feelings about oneself, the ratings in elementary school revealed 67 percent of the boys and 60 percent of the girls had high self-regard. By the time the children reached middle school the numbers had decreased slightly for the boys, 56 percent and more sharply for the girls with a 37 percent rating. By high school, only 29 percent of the girls maintained high self-esteem.

While many factors may contribute to this decline, schools certainly have an important role to play in building self-confidence and keeping possibilities open for all students. Research has shown that teacher behavior often reinforces the message that boys are more capable and more important than girls. At all grade levels, for example, boys get more attention from teachers and more positive feedback. One recent study showed that young black girls get the least amount of positive attention from teachers.

Clearly, we must be more diligent in how we interact with all children, making sure that they learn from us in every possible way that we believe in them and know that they can succeed.

We make too much of it; we are men and women in the second place, human beings in the first.

— Olive Schreiner

The test for whether or not you can hold a job should not be the arrangement of your chromosomes.

— Bella Abzug

Purpose

The purpose of this activity is to encourage students to move beyond limiting notions of what's possible for them, and to encourage them to visualize themselves being successful in any field of endeavor regardless of their gender.

Procedure

1.   You can introduce this activity by reading *He Bear, She Bear* by Stan and Jan Berenstain (New York: Random House, 1974) or *William's Doll* by Charlotte Zolotow (New York: Harper & Row, 1972).

Give the students the opportunity to share their thoughts and feelings about the book.

2. Continue the discussion by having the students brainstorm as many jobs or careers as they can and record these on the board or on butcher paper. You might find it helpful to go through the letters of the alphabet looking for jobs that begin with each letter.

3. Next ask the students which of the jobs can be done by both men and women and which ones are only for men or only for women. Record the students' comments by putting a W (women), M (men), or W/M (both) next to each job name.

4. Discuss with your students the jobs that are labeled W/M as being appropriate for both women and men. Find out if they know people who work in these areas and what they think these jobs are like.

   Ask if these jobs have always been done by both men and women or was there a time when it was practiced only by women or only by men.

5. Now tell the students that they are going on a Scavenger Hunt. Be sure they are familiar with the term or explain that a scavenger hunt is a game where you try to find a number of items within a given time frame or before another team does.

   Our scavenger hunt will be finding women who are doing jobs we think are for men and finding men who are doing jobs we think are just for women.

   Explore with your students how they might go about finding these people. Possibilities include:

   • Using a telephone directory.

   • Asking family members, friends and people in the community.

   • Checking with the librarian to see if he or she could help.

   • Contacting a professional association that represents the occupation.

6. Explain that they will be working in teams to complete this project. Points will be given as follows:

   2 points   •   Find the name of a person who works at one of these jobs.

10 points	•	Interview the person by phone or in person to fill out the Scavenger Hunt Interview Form.
20 points	•	Visit the person at their job site and report back to the entire class what you learned. Perhaps you could bring in photographs of the person on the job.
30 points	•	Invite the person to come to class and talk about their job experience.

Agree on how long to provide for the project (1 to 3 weeks). Find as many people as you can within the time frame. The team with the greatest number of points wins.

7. Have the students get into teams and give them some time to plan how they are going to work together to win the scavenger hunt.

8. At the end of the allotted time, have the students report on their findings.

9. Complete the activity with a discussion about what they learned about job opportunities and how this relates to their own possible career choices.

> *The best careers advice given to the young is 'Find out what you like doing best and get someone to pay you for doing it'.*
>
> —Katherine Whitehorn

Scavenger Hunt
Interview Form

1.   What is your name? _____

    _____

2.   What is your occupation? _____

    _____

3.   How long have you been doing this kind of work? _____

    _____

4.   What kind of qualifications or training do you need for this job?

    _____

    _____

5.   What do you like most about your job? _____

    _____

    _____

6.   What do you like least about your job? _____

    _____

    _____

7.   What advice do you have for young people who might be thinking

    about this as a career? _____

    _____

    _____

    _____

39

From Victim To Leader

> ***V**ictim status not only confers the moral superiority of innocence. It enables people to avoid taking responsibility for their own behavior.*
>
> —John Taylor

Background

The language that we use to describe ourselves and the events in our lives plays a primary role in shaping how we perceive and experience ourselves and our lives.

When the AIDS epidemic hit, people who were infected with the virus were commonly referred to as "victims" of the disease. A further distinction was made by labeling some people as "innocent victims" as if others who had AIDS were "guilty victims."

Since being a victim is the exact opposite of empowerment, it became vitally important to transform the way people talked about the disease. The preferred term became "People Living With AIDS," which allowed for the possibility that not everyone who was infected would die and that, while alive, people with AIDS still maintained their inalienable rights to life, liberty and the pursuit of happiness.

In many ways America has become a society of victims. Consider the so-called "Twinkie defense" used by Dan White, who claimed that he was a victim of temporary insanity caused by eating junk food, and thus was not responsible for killing San Francisco Mayor George Moscone and Supervisor Harvey Milk. A similar insanity defense was used by Nancy Berchtold who sought to be excused from killing her baby because she said she was suffering from postpartum psychosis.

More and more Americans from all walks of life, all cultures, ages and incomes seem to be adopting the status of victim: victims of "dysfunctional families," victims of "codependent relationships," victims of addictions, victims of economic indicators, and victims of teachers' low expectations, governmental graft, bureaucratic boondoggles, professional malpractices, racism, sexism, ageism, homophobia and so forth.

This is not to deny that these conditions exist and need to be changed. The trick is to engage in the process of transforming society from a place of power rather than pain, responsibility rather than resentment, and collaboration rather than condemnation.

Purpose

The purpose of this activity and the next is to challenge students to accept responsibility for living in a world that needs hope, healing and healthy alternatives, and to feel empowered by the opportunities this provides for them to make a real difference.

Procedure

1.   Introduce this activity by asking:

     What is the difference between being a leader and being a victim?

2.   Define "leader" for class:

     Leaders are people who are leaders of themselves. They listen to their own hearts and minds and act accordingly. Others may or may not choose to follow them. A leader is not a true leader until he or she becomes a leader of self. Leaders take responsibility for their actions.

3.   Define "victim" for class:

     Victims are people who are controlled by other people's thoughts and actions and are easily led and persuaded. Helpless as babies, they seem to have no control over what happens to them and are at the mercy of everyone else. Victims rarely take responsibility for themselves and seem to be totally helpless.

4.   Read to the class the following examples of victim situations (or use your own). Then have the class change the situations to examples of leadership situations.

     a.   *Jamie is missing her homework. She says that she did it but her dog ate it when she wasn't looking, so it's not her fault that she doesn't have her homework. How would Jamie act differently if she acted as a responsible leader?*

          Possible answers: 1) After finding her homework missing, Jamie rushes to school a little early and redoes it; 2) Jamie stays in at recess or lunch and does her homework again.

b. *Ronnie is the new boy in class who doesn't know his multiplication tables and keeps making mistakes in class. The popular kids are making fun of Ronnie behind his back. Alex, who wishes he were more popular, starts making fun of Ronnie, too. How would Alex act if he acted as a responsible leader?*

Possible answers: 1) Alex takes his own extra time to teach Ronnie his multiplication tables at recess, lunch, or after school; 2) Alex asks the teacher if he can tutor or drill Ronnie during class time on multiplication tables.

c. *Melissa, a 6th grader, invites her best friend Krista over to play. A five-year-old neighbor, Joshua, is visiting her, too. Krista accidentally drops and breaks Joshua's radio. Krista decides to take it home to see if her father can fix it. Two weeks later, Krista hands the still-broken radio to Melissa at school and tells Melissa to give it to Joshua. Melissa, embarrassed, gives the broken radio back to Joshua and is very angry at Krista because it's still not fixed and Krista is the one that broke it. What could Melissa have done differently if she acted as a responsible leader?*

Possible answers: 1) Melissa could go to her parents and Joshua's parents, explain what happened and enlist her parents to help repair the radio; 2) the same as No. 1 above and include Krista and her parents; 3) Krista and Melissa could save their money and buy another radio for Joshua.

5. Again, ask the class:

What is the difference between being a leader and being a victim?

Ask the class for examples of past situations where they saw someone or themselves acting as a leader of self.

Follow-Up Activities

1. For the rest of the week, have students watch for any situations that make them feel like helpless victims and change the situation so that they become leaders and create their own happy endings.

2. Have students share their personal experiences of changing a victim situation to a leader situation by writing a short story on what happened.

40

From Vision To Action

> *A vision without a task is but a dream,*
> *a task without a vision is drudgery,*
> *a vision and a task are the hope of the world.*
>
> —Sign on the wall of a church in England

Purpose

This activity builds on the previous one by encouraging students to become responsible leaders in their community as well as in the classroom.

Procedure

Part One

1. Introduce the activity by reminding students of the difference between "Victim" and "Leader" and by making some of the points presented in the Background section of Activity 39. You may want to refer to a few famous people who did not settle for being victim to difficult childhood situations but rather became victorious over their circumstances.

2. Brainstorm with your class all the things they don't like about the state of the world: unemployment, homelessness, poverty, crime, starvation, war, drugs and so on.

3. Ask the students to think about which of the bad things in the world has had the most impact on them personally; which ones, if any, they have had to deal with directly at home, at school, in their neighborhood or community.

    Decide on the best way for your students to share their experiences:

- In a letter to themselves, to you, to someone they want to help, to someone they want to forgive, or to someone they think can do something about the situation.

- In a drawing illustrating the circumstances that concerns them.

- In a collage cutting out pictures and words from magazines that illustrate the conditions they want to change.

- In pairs, sharing with a classmate about the situation and how they feel about it.

- In their support groups.

However you structure it, be sure that the students feel safe, have them agree to confidentiality, and remind them that, as always, they are free to pass if they prefer not to share.

4.   After the students have had an opportunity to share their experiences in whatever format you selected, bring the students together again as a full group and ask them to share the insights that they gained from the activity thus far.

Part Two

1.   Next, tell the students that one way of moving from feeling like a VICTIM of these circumstances to feeling more like a LEADER is to create a vision of a better world and to dedicate themselves to doing something to bring this positive vision to life.

Ask the students to write, draw or talk with their partner or support group about what their vision is of a better world.

2.   Once again, bring the entire class together and invite those who are willing to share their vision.

Part Three

1.   Have the students write, draw and talk about what they could do to help make their vision of a better world come true.

For example, if hunger is an area of concern, then the students might consider starting a school-wide drive to collect canned goods to donate to a local soup kitchen. If crime is a concern, then they might vow to be honest and not cheat or steal.

2.   Complete the activity by having students return to the class circle and share what they are going to do to make a positive difference

and how they feel about it. The process, of course, doesn't end here. Encourage students to actually carry out their plans, and provide future opportunities for the students to report back to the class on their accomplishments.

One approach is to have the class choose one project to work together. (Refer to Activity 73, Community Service Projects for further ideas.)

41

Power Full

> ***M**ake the best use of what is in your power, and take the rest as it happens.*
>
> —Epictetus

Purpose

This activity is designed to support students in experiencing a greater sense of potency and inner strength that they can tap into when they want to achieve a goal.

Procedure

1. Have the students sit around in a circle. Suggest to them that each of us has within ourselves a source of power. Tell them that the purpose of this activity is for them to feel their own inner strength.

2. Ask them to close their eyes and imagine a place in their bodies where they will find their source of power.

    With your eyes closed, connect with the spot within your body from which your inner strength and power will come.

    Maybe you are noticing that it is coming from your heart or the top of your head or the palms of your hands or the bottom of your feet.

    There is no right place for it to be. Wherever it is for you is fine.

    Once you have located your source of power, imagine that it is a source of light, warm, clear, pure light.

    Now, let the light get brighter and grow so that it is expanding to fill more and more of your body. Continue until the light has grown to fill your entire body. When you feel that your entire body is full of light, and full of your personal power, please open your eyes.

3.   If some students finish before others, ask them to wait quietly until everyone has opened their eyes.

4.   Give the students an opportunity to share what the experience was like for them.

5.   Next have the students identify an upcoming event at which they are looking to perform well — play well at a ball game, dance well at a recital, present themselves well at a speech, do well on a test, and so forth.

6.   Now, while thinking about their goal, have them close their eyes once again and recreate their source of light expanding to fill their bodies with that power to succeed.

7.   Encourage your students to repeat this process each time they intend to succeed at something.

Chapter Five   *Suggested Student Readings*

BERENSTAIN, STAN AND JAN BERENSTAIN. *He Bear, She Bear.* New York: Random House, 1974.

LARRICK, NANCY. *City Streets.* New York: M. Evans & Co., Inc., 1968.

MERRIAM, EVE. *Mommies at Work.* New York: Simon and Schuster, 1989.

SILVERSTEIN, SHEL. *A Light in the Attic.* New York: Harper & Row, 1981.

TAN, AMY AND GRETCHEN SHIELDS. *The Moon Lady.* New York: Macmillan, 1992.

UCHIDA, YOSHIKO. *The Best Bad Thing.* New York: Antheneum Press, 1983.

VIORST, JUDITH. *Alexander and the Terrible, Horrible, No Good, Very Bad Day.* New York: Antheneum Press, 1972.

ZEMACH, MARGOT. *It Could Always Be Worse.* New York: Scholastic, 1976.

ZOLOTOW, CHARLOTTE. *William's Doll.* New York: Harper & Row, 1972.

CHAPTER SIX

Achievement

Celebrating Success

Accomplishments have no color.

—Leontyne Price

Introduction

Achievement in school is typically defined solely in academic terms which often seem to students to be unrelated to their day-to-day experiences. As New York humorist Fran Lebowitz quipped, "In real life there is no such thing as algebra."

This chapter seeks to motivate students by having them set goals for themselves, and then giving them the skills needed to make their dreams reality. They will learn the importance of envisioning success as well as the power of choosing results over excuses.

Furthermore, students will come to appreciate that there is more than just one way of being smart. Intelligence comes in many forms, and each of us has our own set of strengths and talents that can be developed and applied toward building successful careers and productive lives.

42

Success is . . .

> *Success is getting what you want.*
> *Happiness is wanting what you get.*
>
> — Anonymous

Background

Why do some students succeed in school, while others fail? Theories abound. What is most intriguing is that there are students who succeed despite all odds. They are able to transcend what for most are debilitating circumstances. What is the secret to their motivation?

It is useful to consider human motivation as an analysis—conscious or not—of the costs versus the benefits of any given endeavor. After we weigh the investment required and the risks involved against the potential benefits, if the benefits outweigh the costs we are motivated to act. If the costs are too great and without sufficient payoff, we will not pursue a particular course of action.

All students must invest to a certain degree in order to achieve success. Attending classes rather than hanging out with friends, studying rather than listening to music, risking giving the wrong answer—these are all costs.

Students who receive encouragement and rewards at home and also imagine long-term rewards in terms of greater career opportunities are likely to think that the benefits are worth the effort. Intrinsically motivated students, for whom the joy of learning and the personal feeling of accomplishment are their own rewards, are also likely to make the investment.

Making that effort is more difficult, however, for students whose family and community show little evidence that school success is the road to better jobs and improved quality of life. Add to that a peer culture in which being good in school is seen as selling out, and you've increased the cost and reduced the benefits considerably.

If these costs are compounded by a school experience of being excluded and devalued, then, clearly, the costs will appear too great and the payoffs too small to justify the effort.

Although schools may not be able to influence the job situation in today's economy, they can help eliminate barriers for women and people of color by developing in today's students—the next generation of citizens—a greater appreciation for and celebration of diversity.

In the short term, schools can create learning environments where students—all students—feel included, where the curriculum reflects the struggles and strengths of all peoples, and where all students are esteemed for being who they are.

In this activity, students are asked to define success. You might ask them to consider the costs and benefits of success. What are some of the ways students resist school—misbehavior, vandalism, dropping out, and so forth. What would make the education exchange worth it? How can they maintain their sense of self and sense of cultural identity—and still succeed?

Purpose

For students to explore what is meant by success — how achievement is defined by society, their culture, their family, their peers and themselves.

Procedure

1. Write the word *success* on the board and ask the students what it means. Write down their responses on butcher paper divided into sections — our class, our friends, our families, our society.

2. Continue to explore the idea of *success* by asking the class how society at large defines success. What images are projected in the media, for example, of success? What kinds of people are spotlighted as being successful?

    • Ask the students what their parents and families think of as being successful.

    • Now see what their friends and peers mean by success. Do they have the same values as families and society? Discuss commonalities and variations.

- How about the students' personal definition of success? How influenced are they by these other groups?

- Discuss the relationship between *success* and *happiness*. How are these the same or different? Can someone be happy and not successful? Successful but not happy?

3.   Have the students move into teams to write a composite poem that captures each of their personal definitions of success.

Each student says what success means to him or her, and then the teams weaves these thoughts together into a poem.

While they could write their poem in free verse, it might be more fun if they tried to make it rhyme.

4.   When the teams are finished, have them read their poems to the rest of the class. You may want to have them printed on large paper to post in the classroom. The students could also draw on their posters to illustrate their poems of success.

Variation

Depending upon how extensive a list of definitions of success were identified, you may want to extend this activity over a period of a few days. Before doing procedure 3 and 4, invite students to continue to explore what success means by paying attention to TV, interviewing family and friends, and so forth.

43

Success Collage

> *To follow, without halt, one aim: there's the secret of success.*
>
> —Anna Pavlova

Purpose

When you dream of success, what do you see? Do you imagine yourself winning the lottery? Do you see yourself in a position of power and influence? Do you have a picture of your ideal home and family? Or do you dream of making an enduring mark in the world? Or being remembered for your contribution to humanity?

One secret to being successful is to have a clear picture of what success looks like for you . The next two activities are designed to have your students develop detailed pictures of what they want in the way of success and happiness.

Materials

Heavy drawing paper (12 x 18 inches)
Magazines (including foreign language if possible)
Scissors
Glue or paste

Procedure

1. Distribute to students the drawing paper, magazines, scissors and glue. They may work in teams to share some of the materials.

2. Tell students to look through the magazines and find pictures of things that suggest what they personally think of as success and happiness.

3. Have them cut out pictures and glue them on the paper in designs that represent their personal views of success and happiness.

4. Suggest that they include words or phrases that fit into their designs. If there are other images they want to include that they can't find in magazines, they are free to draw them.

5. When the students have completed their collages, have them take turns showing the others their collages and explaining how the designs illustrate their ideas of happiness and success. The other team members may ask questions if anything on a design seems unclear.

6. You may want to close the activity with a full class discussion along the following lines: "Look again at the collage you created. Of all the images you used in the design, which is most important to you?"

7. You may want to invite your students to take their collages home, and find time to discuss them with their parents. The collage can be used as a starting point for them to let their parents know what their current life goals are.

    You may also want to make the following suggestions: "Ask your parents to tell you what their goals were when they were your age. Then find out what they would like to see for your future. See if your goals and your parents' goals for you match."

8. Ask your students to bring the collages back to class so that they can be displayed on the bulletin board.

44

Highlights of My Life II

You must do the thing you think you cannot do.

—Eleanor Roosevelt

Purpose

The purpose of this activity is for students to create a vision of what they would like to accomplish in the future.

Procedure

1. You could do this activity solely as a worksheet exercise, using the same process as Activity 15, only this time asking the students to project 15 years into the future.

2. It could be done first as a guided visualization.

3. Introduce the activity by explaining what students will be doing:

    This activity is an eyes-closed, guided visualization. You will be in your favorite room watching a video of your life as it might be in the future. It is an opportunity for you to begin creating a successful future for yourself.

4. Ask students to close their eyes, relax, and take a few deep breaths.

5. Continue with the following instructions:

    You find yourself walking down a hallway that feels like home.

At the end of the hallway, you discover a room just like the one you've always wanted.

As you enter the room, you notice the colors in the room —the walls, the floor, the furniture. You also notice that all your favorite things are in this room, and you realize this is really a perfect place to be.

And now you decide to find a place where you can relax for a few minutes—maybe a comfortable chair or sofa, or perhaps a bed or a stack of pillows on the floor.

As you get really comfortable, you decide to watch TV for awhile, and as you do, you notice a television set and you see that you have a good view of it from where you are sitting. . . . Very good!

As the television comes on, you see the title of a movie, "Coming Attractions."

Your future is divided into three parts:

- *the next five years,*

- *the five years after that, and*

- *the five years after that.*

So you are reviewing the next 15 years of your life. You'll be seeing the highlights of your life—the major events or accomplishments that will occur during this time. Some of the events you may experience are:

- *completing elementary school and high school*

- *getting your driver's license and being able to drive a car.*

*And now, as you continue to look and listen, notice what events unfold
in your life.*

If the screen goes blank or isn't clear, that's okay. Just ask yourself, 'What will I accomplish in my life during the next five years?' and listen to the answers. Let it flow easily. And as you do, you notice that you can see and hear many events you would like to have occur in the next five years.

(Pause for two to four minutes.)

And now you find yourself drifting even further into the future. You are beginning to move on to the next five years—6 to 10 years from now. Excellent! Very good!

By now you have probably been in high school or have graduated high school and have gone on to college or a full–time job.

(Use age-appropriate information here.)

And, as you take your next breath, you begin to notice what high points might occur during this period of your life.

And, as I stop talking, you begin to see and hear what shows up on your screen.

(Pause for two to four minutes.)

Very good. . . . As you let go of these images, you begin to find yourself moving on to the 10- to 15-year range, so you might notice in the mirror how you've gotten a little older. You may be surprised at how much older and more mature you look!

During this time frame, you will be approaching and maybe passing 20 years of age. What will you have accomplished by now?

- *enjoying a significant relationship*

- *living on your own*

- *a new, more challenging job*

- *maybe you've become famous for something.*

Just let yourself continue to watch the screen and notice what you see ahead.

(Pause for two to four minutes.)

Very good. Now, as you begin to let go of these sounds and images, you find your awareness leaving the television set and coming back to the room. You realize that for now the movie is over. There'll be more to see later in the future, but it is time to leave now. So you get up and turn off the TV.

As you get ready to leave the room, you realize that you can always return here to go back to your future any time you want, simply by closing your eyes and walking down the hall, but for now it is time to leave.

As you leave and walk back down the hall, you realize what a gift it is to be clear about some of your visions for the future.

After awhile, you find yourself walking down the hallway to this classroom. As you enter the room, you take your seat and begin to notice how it feels to sit in your chair. You can feel your back against the back of the chair and your feet on the floor. As you notice the rising and falling of your chest and stomach as you breathe in and out, you become aware of the sounds around you in the room. You start to think about what this room looks like. When you have a clear sense of it, you slowly open your eyes and return your attention to the room.

6. Hand out copies of the worksheet, Highlights of My Life II, and have the students write or draw in the filmstrip frames images of their future success that they experienced during the fantasy.

7. Have the students share with partners or in their support groups.

8. Bring the entire class together for final comments.

Highlights of My Life II Worksheet

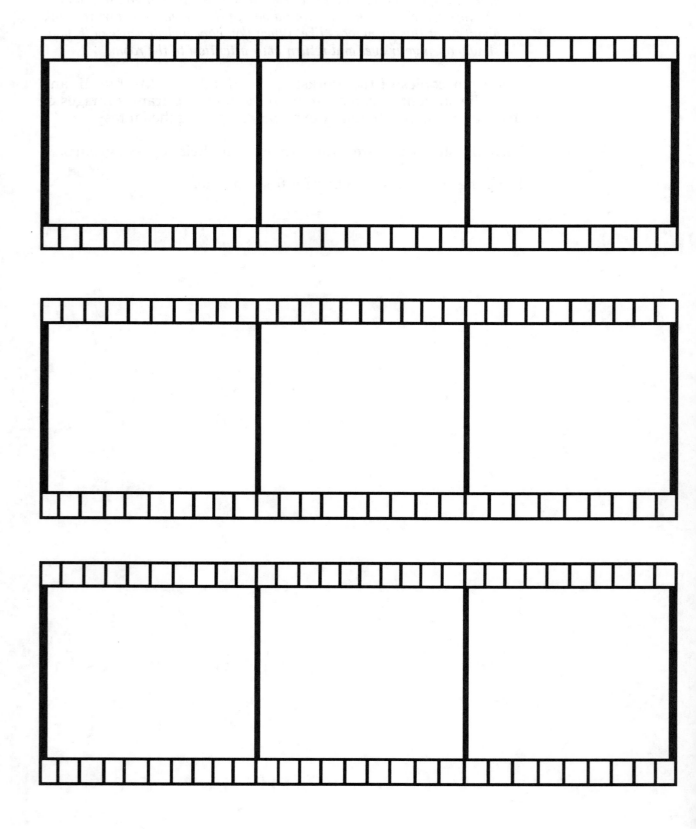

45

Favorite Excuses

We *are all manufacturers — making good, making trouble or making excuses.*

—H. V. Adolt

Purpose

This activity helps students to realize that they can either have what they want in life (their goals), or they can have the excuses for why they don't have what they want.

"The dog ate my homework."
"The car broke down."
"My mother didn't wake me up in time."
"Somebody stole my pencil."
"Nobody told me!"

Do you recognize these? They are famous favorite excuses that every kid learns along with the ABCs. Everybody has a sackful of excuses, good for any occasion. What's your excuse? (And don't try to use the excuse that you couldn't think of an excuse!)

Materials

Post-it® pads

Procedure

1. Have the students bring their chairs into a class circle.

2. Give them each a stack of Post-it® Notes.

3.   Tell them that they are going to be writing excuses on the Post-it®
Notes, one excuse per note.

4.   Instruct them as follows:

*First write all the excuses you can think of for not getting your
homework done. Remember, one excuse per note.*

Next, write all the excuses you know for not getting to school on time.

Now all the excuses for not taking out the garbage.

Now all the ones for not cleaning your room.

All the excuses you have for not liking yourself.

All the excuses you have for others not liking you.

All the excuses for not doing well in school.

All the excuses for not finishing your 24-hour goal.

5.   Go around the circle and have students read off their favorite
excuses and post them on a "Favorite Excuses" bulletin board.

6.   You may want to explore with your students what motivates
people to settle for the excuse rather than succeed at a goal. What
purpose does excuse-making serve?

Sometimes excuses are ways we have of protecting ourselves. We
protect ourselves from the discomfort of feeling like a failure if we
have a good excuse for not having met our goal. We can avoid the
fear of punishment if we can convince our parents that we had a
good enough reason for not doing what we were told. We can save
face with our friends if we can blame our parents for not letting us
stay out all night.

7.   In the future, when a student gives an excuse for something, you
can simply point to the "Favorite Excuses" bulletin board and
suggest that it is not necessary to make up a new one—that we
already have plenty from which to pick. Remind them that *you can
have what you want (your goal) or you can have the excuses why you
don't.*

Note: *This activity often raises the question as to whether there are ever "legitimate
excuses." The term excuse is being used here to describe those times when people
settle for less than they are capable of achieving and point to something outside
themselves as the reason why.*

The activity is meant to challenge that mindset in order to empower students by having them realize they need not be limited by circumstances. In this sense, it is related to Activity 39, From Victim to Leader. The key is personal responsibility. There are times when I deliberately choose to do something other than what I said I would do. (My grandmother came to visit and I chose to spend time with her rather than do my homework. My relationships goal became more important than my achievement goal. I chose it. I am not making an excuse for myself. I am willing to accept the consequences of my actions.)

Other times, circumstances beyond my control prevent me from achieving what I set out to do. ("I agreed to meet you at 4:00pm to play ball and the bus was late. When I made the agreement, I didn't plan for such an eventuality. Knowing what I know about public transportation, I should have left earlier, arranged for other transportation or told you 4:30pm instead. I apologize for keeping you waiting. In the future, I'll plan better.") Once again, responsibility leads to empowerment.

46

I Can't / I Haven't Yet

> *If you think you can, you can. And if you think you can't, you're right.*
>
> —Mary Kay Ash

Purpose

To support students in realizing how language affects their perception, and how they can use responsible statements to empower themselves.

Procedure

1. Ask the students to find partners. Have them take turns saying sentences that feel true for them that start with the words "I can't . . ."— for example, "I can't learn to do math," "I can't remember my times tables," "I can't get to school on time," "I can't make any friends." Ask them to consider their school life, their social life, their home life, and so on as possible areas from which to draw these statements.

2. After about two minutes, ask them to go back and repeat all the sentences they have just said with one change: replacing the word "can't" with the words "haven't yet," such as "I haven't yet learned how to do math"; "I haven't yet remembered my times tables"; and so forth.

   Ask them to repeat exactly what they said before except for the substitution of "haven't yet" for "can't," and to take the time to be aware of how they experience saying each sentence. Ask them to notice if it feels any different, and, if it does, to remember how it feels different. Again, give them about two minutes to do this.

3. Bring the class back together and ask them what they experienced as they did the exercise. Did they experience any difference between saying "I can't" and "I haven't yet"?

4. Ask them to consider whether their "I can't" statements are really statements of something that is impossible, or whether it is something possible that they simply have not yet done. "I can't" implies being unable, limited, and controlled from the outside. "I haven't yet" creates the possibility that it can happen now or sometime in the future.

5. After you have used this exercise with your class, make a habit of correcting people in class who say, "I can't." Ask them to repeat whatever they have said with the words "I haven't yet."

47

Intention Versus Mechanism

> **L**ife is like playing a violin in public and learning the instrument as one goes along.
>
> —Samuel Butler

Purpose

The point of this exercise is for students to discover that most things do not happen by accident. They will discover that intention, the determination to go after a chosen goal, is more important than mechanism, the method used in achieving the goal; and that there are many different ways of solving a problem or reaching a goal.

Procedure

1.   Begin the lesson with:

     What do you think is more important in reaching your goals: intention, which is what you want to do, or mechanism, which is the way you want to do it?

     Have students vote for the one they think is more important.

     Today we will find out which is more important.

2.   Students form a circle of chairs facing inward, with two openings opposite each other.

3.   All students stand together outside the circle at one of its openings.

4.   Next, explain to the students:

The object of this activity is to start from one opening of the circle and go across to the opposite opening. Each of you must do this, one at a time, using a different way or mechanism to get across. No two people can use the same method to get across.

5.   Choose a student to demonstrate one way of going across the circle. (Probably, the student will choose to walk across. Other methods might be hopping, skipping, sidestepping, or dancing.)

6.   While upbeat music is playing (optional), the rest of the class follows the first student, going one at a time. Stress that each student must use a different method. After students go through, they take seats in the circle.

7.   After everyone has finished, have a class discussion on key points:

   a.   *How many different ways did we find to get across the circle?*

   b.   *Why is intention more important than the mechanism, or method?*

   c.   *Goals are reached by clear intention and not by accident. (Be sure to stress this.)*

   d.   *What are some goals that the class can reach by having a clear intention?*

Note: *This exercise may be done as an outside activity.*

Follow-Up Activity

For a follow-up lesson have students list a particular goal and identify a variety of possible mechanisms (solutions) for achieving that goal.

48

Report Card Affirmation

---

*I*ntelligence is characterized by a natural inability to understand.

— Henri Bergson

Background

Affirmations are positive statements that affirm or declare a desired objective as if it were already achieved. The purpose of an affirmation is to build "structural tension" or "cognitive dissonance" in the brain, which thereby creates the internal motivation to take the necessary actions required to achieve a goal. This structural tension can be further increased by using the affirmation in conjunction with a clear visual image of the desired outcome.

Whenever the mind simultaneously holds two realities that do not match, cognitive dissonance occurs. If your current reality is that you are a poor student and you affirm and visualize being an excellent student, then you will experience structural tension. If you deliberately create and hold this structural tension in your mind on a daily basis, it will intensify and create the following mental changes:

- You will begin to experience creative ideas that will help you achieve your goal.

- You will start to perceive all kinds of internal and external resources to help you achieve your goal that you were never aware of before now. Your awareness will expand to take in new data to help you.

- You will experience increased motivation to take action.

All motivation comes from having a picture of something you want that does not match the picture of what you have. The more you can increase the interplay between those two images, the more you will increase your motivation. Affirmations, which are word pictures describing the completed goal, help elicit visual pictures, thus increasing the structural tension and motivation.

The beliefs, expectations, and thought patterns that your students currently hold also determine their self-esteem, and how willing they are to participate in school and in life. If students believe that they are slow learners, poor students, not mathematically inclined, physically awkward, or stupid, then that is what they will create. The belief and the picture will create the future and will control their actions.

Students can learn to use affirmations to override their self-defeating beliefs. They can transform their internal experience of themselves, and then gradually modify their daily behavior to match their new beliefs.

Purpose

This exercise works on the principle of "cognitive dissonance" applied to student's academic achievement. The purpose is to motivate students to improve their performance whether measured by grades or some other means of assessment.

Materials

Blank report card forms (14 per student)
An envelope for each student

Procedure

1.   Give each student 14 blank report card forms.

2.   Instruct each student to take one copy of the form and write down all the necessary information: his or her name, classes, teachers, and so on.

3.   In cases where grades are used, have the students think about what grades they would like to see on their report cards. Make the point that the grades don't necessarily have to be straight A's. Tell your students to write in the grades they want to see on their report cards—"the grade you believe you actually are capable of earning at this point."

4.   If the form of assessment is something other than grades and report cards, then discuss with your students how their performance will

be measured, what skills they are expected to learn, what projects they will be expected to complete, what products will be used to evaluate their progress. Supply students with copies of whatever assessment tool they will actually be receiving, and tell them to fill in the performance objectives they intend to accomplish.

5. Have them bring their completed report cards or assessment forms with them to share with the entire group.

6. After they have shown their report cards or assessment forms to the class, ask them to agree to repeat this activity — writing out forms with the grades or alternative measures of success they want to see on their next performance record — twice a day for the next five days.

7. Have the students put a copy of their completed form in an envelope and address it to themselves. Collect these envelopes for safe keeping. At the end of the reporting period return the forms to the students and discuss the process.

4 9

Four Thinkers

> *The best teacher is not necessarily the one who possesses the most knowledge, but the one who most effectively enables his students to believe in their ability to learn.*
>
> —Norman Cousins

Purpose

Students will recognize four ways of thinking about goals and practice the one that leads to success.

Procedure

1.   Begin by saying:

      We are going to find out about four different ways of thinking. Some of you will come up and role-play the thinkers. Listen and watch, and then find out what kind of thinker you are and what kind of thinker you want to be.

2.   Draw the following diagram on the board. (In the diagram, a star ★ is used to indicate *goals*. A box ■ is used to indicate a *problem* or an *obstacle*.)

3.   Explain No. 4 Thinkers:

No. 4 Thinkers have no goals, no ambition, and few wants. They are bored and boring. (Point to the empty space where the star would be on the diagram.)

4.   Role-play a No. 4 Thinker. Have one student act out this thinker by sitting in a chair and staring at an imaginary TV in a dull, boring manner. Nothing can get this thinker excited. Choose three or four students to come up to the No. 4 Thinker and try to get this thinker excited about something. Possible statements they can make:

— Want to go to the beach?
— I found ten dollars. Let's spend it!
— Let's go ride bikes.

Another name for this type of thinker is "The Stuck One," because being glued to the TV, this thinker doesn't experience life completely.

5.   Explain No. 3 Thinkers:

No. 3 Thinkers are called "Spaghetti Brains" because they are confused and have goals scattered all over the place: They always want to go somewhere but they never get anywhere. They know they want something, but they don't know what it is. Poor Spaghetti Brains! A boy once got his mother to take him to the public library to work on his country report, but he forgot what country he was doing! No. 3 Thinkers hardly ever get what they want.

6.   Role-play a No. 3 Thinker. Have a student act out Spaghetti Brains in the library with his mother. Have one student role-play his mother and another, the librarian.

The mother says, "What country are you studying?"

Spaghetti Brains: "I can't remember exactly, but I know it starts with the letter S or T or maybe R."

The librarian comes up and asks if he needs help.

Spaghetti Brains: "I'm doing a country report but I can't quite remember which country it's on. I know the name ends with the letter A or G or E or maybe N."

Librarian: "If you don't know which country, I can't help you."

Spaghetti Brains: "Well, maybe you know my teacher, Miss Jones. She's got blonde hair and brown eyes and she gives this assignment every year."

Boy's mother: "You've got to remember the country's name."

Spaghetti Brains: "Well, no, I can't remember but maybe someone in the library right now might have had my teacher before."

The No. 3 Thinker would be just as well off if he was at home eating spaghetti.

7.   Explain No. 2 Thinkers: No. 2 Thinkers only think about the problems or the obstacles and complain a lot. "Yeah, But" is this thinker's nickname. All the problems get bigger and bigger until the No. 2 Thinkers themselves become the problem. If they're not the problem, they're out looking for the problems. The No. 2 Thinkers live on an obstacle course. Draw boxes on the No. 2 Thinker on the diagram in another color chalk.

8.   Role-play a No. 2 Thinker. The No. 2 Thinker can be acted out by a student who is good at complaining because he or she finds something wrong with everything and everybody.

Scene: class is planning a party. Everyone makes suggestions about the party. After every suggestion, "Yeah, But" might say:

— Yeah, but it's too expensive.
— Yeah, but there's not enough time.
— Yeah, but it's not fun.
— Yeah, but we need more boys.
— Yeah, but we need more food.
— Yeah, but we never planned a party before.

"Yeah, But" is big on finding obstacles.

9.   Explain No. 1 Thinkers: No. 1 Thinkers get what they want. Their eyes are always on the goal. If a problem or an obstacle comes up, they just see it as a challenge or an opportunity, and it gets them excited. No. 1 Thinkers have goals, aim for the stars and follow their dreams. Stick with the No. 1 Thinker and you'll make things happen.

10.   Role-play a No. 1 Thinker. Have the class pick something reasonable that they would like to do, such as cooking, a special art activity, a local field trip to the park, and so forth. The class must convince the teacher that this activity is worthwhile by answering every doubt or question the teacher has. Meanwhile, the teacher takes on the roles of No. 2, 3, and 4 Thinkers and comes up with every possible excuse or obstacle. The students' goal is to never give up, answer each of the teacher's questions, and work through every obstacle. As each obstacle comes up, students should identify which kind of thinker it represents.

11.   Divide the class into groups of three or four. Each group meets and picks one personal goal. Examples: have a special activity in class, watch a video at lunch, tutor a first grader, and so forth. Challenge each group to be No. 1 Thinkers and meet their goals. Encourage them to work through all obstacles and work as a team. Have one person in each group be a recorder and record all the different solutions they try until they reach their goal.

Note: *Ham it up and use your own explanations to clarify as needed. Divide the lesson into two parts if it's too long. It can also be made into a four-act play and performed for another class.*

50

Using All My Smarts

> *Even the best needles are not sharp at both ends.*
>
> —Chinese Proverb

Background

As public schools struggle to serve an increasingly diverse student population, a growing number of youngsters are identified as being "at risk." An alternative view is that it is the schools, not the students, that are "at risk" — at risk of failing to provide for the needs of their clients. Shifting the focus in this way challenges schools to find alternatives for serving all students, not just those who are able to adapt to the existing educational pedagogy and methodology.

For example, most schools favor a mode of instruction that is individualistic and highly competitive. European American males tend to have an advantage in this type of environment, whereas females and members of other cultural groups are more likely to succeed in a cooperative group setting.

Recognizing that students have different learning styles is a necessary first step in transforming "at risk" schools. Many different theories of learning styles exist and the exact way in which culture, ethnicity, social class, and child-rearing practices influence learning styles is not completely clear. However, using a range of different teaching styles in order to engage students in a manner that is likely to be compatible with their style of learning is an obvious approach that holds great promise.

Howard Gardner's work on multiple intelligences, though not specifically related to cultural differences, is one theory that has important implications because it goes beyond the limited definition of intelligence valued in most schools.

According to Gardner, people are capable of processing information, solving problems, and developing products in several different ways—each of which could be said to be a specific "intelligence." These include:

- **Verbal / Linguistic**
  Referring to the use of words and language both written and spoken, this intelligence is the basis for reading, writing, abstract reasoning, symbolic thinking and so forth. The curriculum of most Western educational systems are dominated by this way of knowing.

- **Logical / Mathematical**
  This is the other predominant intelligence emphasized in most schools. The number skills of the mathematician as well as the reasoning skills of the scientist are included in this domain.

- **Visual / Spatial**
  The sense of sight is key to this intelligence. Being able to visualize objects from different perspectives and create mental pictures are among the skills that are important to the artists, designers, architects and others who have strengths in this type of intelligence.

- **Body / Kinesthetic**
  Athletes and dancers are obvious examples of people who are skilled in this area. "Learning by doing" is the best way to teach the kinesthetic learner.

- **Musical / Rhythmic**
  Music and rhythm are sometimes used to teach younger children such as with the ABCs jingle. According to advocates of "Super Learning," a particular type of background music enhances student ability to learn foreign languages or retain factual information. Composers and musicians exemplify people with skills in this area.

- **Interpersonal**
  This intelligence supports the ability to be effective in dealing with other people. Communication, cooperation and compassion are among the skills of people such as teachers, counselors and therapists who have strengths in this area.

- **Intrapersonal**
  Philosophers perhaps best reflect this intelligence which involves knowledge of the internal aspects of oneself such as observing emotional states and thinking processes, as well as an awareness of spiritual realities.

Purpose

The aim of this activity is to have students become aware of the different ways of knowing. Students who are adept at intelligences that are typically undervalued in schools will feel validated.

In addition, you may feel excited about the challenge of planning your lessons with the seven intelligences* in mind so that all students have an opportunity to build on their strengths.

Procedure

1. Have students get into their teams and give them copies of the All My Smarts Worksheet I.

2. Ask them to identify students within their team who are good at the skills that are listed on the Worksheet. Students may mention their own names as well as those of their teammates.

3. Bring the class together. Review each cluster of strengths and have each team mention students in their group who have these skills.

   Write each skill on the board and put in the names or initials of students who are strong in these areas.

   After each cluster of skills, identify the area of intelligence to which these belong by writing the heading on the board.

4. Next give each student a copy of All My Smarts Worksheet II and ask them to color in the parts that show their strengths—estimating how fully developed each skill is. Starting at the center of the circle have them fill in as much of each section as they feel they have this particular set of skills. Some of the students for example may fill in almost all of the athlete wedge, half of the musician wedge and ten percent of the scientist wedge.

5. Now have the students pick one of the type of intelligences that is less developed and make a goal to increase their skill in this area. Discuss with your students what they have already learned from previous activities about achieving goals that they can apply to this area.

6. Make the point that each student has a different set of strengths and that we can learn from each other. Invite the students to mill

---

* For further discussion of multiple intelligences as it relates to educational practices, read *Seven Ways of Teaching* and *Seven Ways of Knowing*, both by David Lazear, Palantine, IL: Skylight Publishing, 1991.

around the classroom talking to their classmates, comparing their All My Smarts Worksheet II charts. Have each student find a "mentor" — someone who is strong in the area that they are weak (targeted as a goal to be developed).

7. Give them time to meet with their mentor to discuss ways in which to improve in this area.

8. Reinforce the relationship by providing time over the next few days and weeks for students to meet with their mentors.

9. In about two weeks have the mentors present their protégés and share with the rest of the class what progress the student has made.

10. Have the students update their charts on the All My Smarts Worksheet II.

All My Smarts Worksheet I

AUTHOR   Skill Set 1   Student's Name
                 • reading/vocabulary   _____
                 • creative writing/poetry   _____
                 • speaking/humor   _____

SCIENTIST   Skill Set 2   Student's Name
                 • math   _____
                 • outlining   _____
                 • figuring out codes
                     and puzzles   _____

ARTIST   Skill Set 3   Student's Name
                 • art   _____
                 • color/design   _____
                 • vivid imagination   _____

ATHLETE   Skill Set 4   Student's Name
                 • sports/martial arts   _____
                 • dance/mime   _____
                 • inventing   _____

MUSICIAN   Skill Set 5   Student's Name
                 • singing   _____
                 • music   _____
                 • vocal sounds   _____

COUNSELOR   Skill Set 6   Student's Name
                 • communication   _____
                 • cooperative learning   _____
                 • caring about others   _____

PHILOSOPHER Skill Set 7   Student's Name
                 • self reflection   _____
                 • focus/concentration   _____
                 • spirituality   _____

All My Smarts Worksheet II

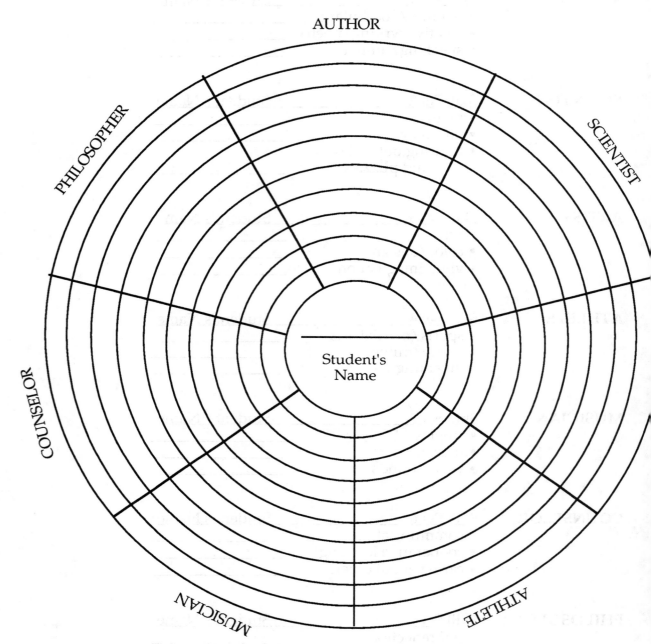

Goal Area _____

Mentor _____

51

Captain Self-Esteem

---

*Y*ou ask me why I do not write something . . . I think one's
feelings waste themselves in words, they ought all to be
distilled into actions and into actions which bring results.

—Florence Nightingale

Anecdotal Material

This activity was done with a group of high school students. They were
told that other teachers in the school were curious about what these
students were learning in the self-esteem program, and so they decided to
produce a video that could be used to communicate what we had been
doing. They were given thirty minutes to prepare.

When the students returned; lights, camera, action!

The students role-played being at a party. Each of them had a sign
indicating how they were feeling — bored, lonely, sad, upset, and so forth
— as they acted out these feelings.

After much complaining and negative commentary, someone finally said,
"This looks like a job for Captain Self-Esteem." In came this hefty young
man with a big 'S' on his shirt to save the day.

As Captain Self-Esteem touched each of the students, they turned their
signs around — bored changed to having fun, lonely became friendly, sad
turned to happy and so forth — and proceeded to act consistent with
these positive feelings.

The selection of this particular student as Captain Self-Esteem—however
the students decided upon it—was brilliant because he was the member of
the group most in need of learning to value himself and experience the
acceptance of others.

Purpose

To support students in integrating the key learnings of this section by asking them to apply their knowledge in some type of presentation.

Materials

Video recorder and playback equipment
Blank video tape

Procedure

1. Let students know that we have come to the end of another section of the program, and that it is time for the next episode in their TV series.

Creative Approach

2. Hand out the Part III Key Learnings and discuss the points that were covered in these two chapters. Have the students vote on the one or more ideas they would like to use in this activity.

3. Review with your students possible types of television programs (e.g. news, talk shows, music videos, award shows, drama, comedy, and so forth), and decide with them what form to use in relation to the topics selected.

4. Give them time to work on the concept, write the script, make props, rehearse, and so forth.

5. Proceed to Step 10 below.

Structured Approach

2. Borrowing the idea from the students mentioned in the Anecdotal Material, tell your students that the title of the TV episode is "Captain Self-Esteem."

3. Brainstorm with your students a list of words describing how people feel when they don't have any self-esteem, when they don't feel empowered or don't feel successful.

4. Next, have students identify words that describe how people feel when they do have self-esteem. A good way of doing this would be to have the negative feeling in one column and the opposite, positive feeling in a column next to it.

5. Have each student select one of the pairs of words (sad/happy, upset/calm, and so forth) that they would be willing to act out. Have them make a sign with the negative word on one side and the positive word on the other. The signs should be large enough to be read by the camera.

6. Describe the set-up: students in a group acting out low self-esteem behaviors; "Captain Self-Esteem" arrives and zaps them with power and confidence; group changes to high self-esteem behaviors.

7. Ask students for suggestions as to how to pick who will play "Captain Self-Esteem." Possible ways of choosing might include:

    - one student volunteers and no one else wants to do it, and everyone is comfortable with his or her having this role,
    - if there is more than one volunteer, then they could audition for the part and students could vote on who did the best job,
    - random selection.

8. Have the group decide on what type of a setting they want to create for the scene — at a party, in a classroom, at a ball game, outside on the playground, and so forth.

9. Give students some time to work together in small groups discussing what kinds of behaviors are appropriate for the "before" as well as the "after" scenes. You are likely to have more students than pairs of words, so more than one student can act out sad/happy for example. You could have students with the same pair of words get together to plan different ways of acting out the part.

10. Do a dress rehearsal and have students offer constructive feedback for how to make it even better.

11. Videotape it and play it back.

12. Discuss with the students whether or not they would like to show the video to anyone else.

13. Complete the activity with a discussion on what the students have learned so far in the program.

Low Self-Esteem Feelings and Actions	High Self-Esteem Feelings and Actions
mad	glad
sad	happy
upset	calm
lonely	friendly
bored	excited, having fun
victim	victor
complaining	complementing
withdrawing	participating
arguing	communicating
failing	succeeding
making excuses	excelling

Part III—Key Learnings

⚷ I am capable of being
     anything I want to be.

⚷ I am getting what I want
     rather than settling for
     excuses.

⚷ I am able to move from victim
     to responsible leader.

⚷ It is not that I can't, I just
     haven't yet.

⚷ I am capable.

⚷ I am smart.

⚷ I am responsible for how I
     respond to events in my life.

⚷ I think like a winner.

⚷ I have the power to succeed.

⚷ I am achieving my goals.

Part III—Teacher Checklist
Creating a Respectful and Responsible Learning Environment

❑ Am I tailoring my curriculum so that it is relevant to my students—their interests, ambitions, as well as their cultural identity?

❑ Am I aware of my students various learning styles, and do my teaching strategies reflect this?

❑ Are the books and other materials I use reflective of diversity —ethnicity, culture, race, class, gender, age, handicapping conditions, and so forth?

❑ Are the images on the walls and bulletin boards also reflective of diversity?

❑ Are a variety of family groupings, lifestyles and types of homes represented in my classroom materials?

❑ Are the materials in my classroom nonsexist—showing both males and females in nurturing roles and depicting a variety of occupational roles and interest areas as being equally appropriate for girls and boys?

❑ How is the seating arrangement consistent with my educational objectives, and how does it support all students in learning most effectively?

❑ Have I provided opportunities for my students to help maintain the classroom environment so as to encourage their sense of responsibility?

❑ Were the students involved in developing class rules (operating instructions, protocol or agreements) so that they feel ownership for them?

❑ Do I give my students opportunities to make choices in appropriate areas as a way of letting them exercise responsibility?

❑ Have all my students set goals for themselves and am I providing effective coaching that may be different for each child but equally empowering for all of them?

Chapter Six   *Suggested Student Readings*

CUMMINGS, PAT. *Jimmy Lee Did It.* New York: Lothrop, 1985.

DOBRIN, ARNOLD. *Josephine's Magination.* New York: Scholastic, 1975.

DR. SEUSS. *Horton Hatches the Egg.* New York: Random House, 1940.

FELT, SUSAN. *Rosa Too Little.* New York: Doubleday, 1950.

LITTLE, LESSIE AND ELOISE GREENFIELD. *I Can Do It Myself.* New York: Crowell, 1978.

MARTIN, BILL JR. AND JOHN ARCHAMBAULT. *Knots on a Counting Rope.* Allen, TX: DCM, 1989.

SHAH, INDRIES. *World Tales.* New York: Harcourt Brace Jovanovich, 1979.

UCHIDA, YOSHIKO. *Sumi's Prize.* New York: Scribner's, 1964.

WISNIEWSKI, DAVID. *Rain Player.* New York: Clarion Books, 1991.

PART IV

RESPECT FOR OTHERS AND SOCIAL RESPONSIBILITY

Making the World Work

How wonderful it is that nobody need wait a single moment before starting to improve the world.

—Anne Frank

	Experience (Internal)	Express (External)
Others	Interdependence	Social Responsibility
Self	Independence	Personal Responsibility

CHAPTER SEVEN

Collaboration

Can't We All Get Along?

A generous heart feels others' ills as if it were responsible for them.

—Vauvenargues

Introduction

Stereotypes, prejudices and discrimination are ways in which people from one group keep themselves separate from and better than another group. Such attitudes and behaviors are based upon ignorance, insecurity and fear. Being on the receiving end of prejudice diminishes one's sense of self-worth, especially if it plays into the recipient's fears and insecurities.

This chapter emphasizes the importance of all us working together. We must all learn to cooperate rather than compete and to move beyond conflict to collaboration.

Students will learn to communicate better—especially to listen to other's viewpoints. They will learn to trust each other and to solve problems together. In this way we can replace ignorance with knowledge, insecurity with confidence, and fear with love.

It is incumbent upon us as educators to model effective communication and listening skills. As the saying goes, "students don't care how much we know until they know how much we care." One of the best ways to show we care is to really listen so that students feel heard.

Communication styles vary among cultural groups, and it is important to be sensitive to these differences. I observed an interaction between an urban elementary school principal who was admonishing a young African American child. The boy had his eyes cast downward as he was listening to the man's harsh words.

Misunderstanding the child's stance, the principal, a Caucasian of Greek descent, grabbed the boy's chin and demanded that he look at him while he was speaking. Ways of showing respect were totally opposite for the two different cultures.

Cultural rules related to communication, such as those listed here, are offered as general guidelines and are by no means meant to stereotype any particular group. Treating each person as an individual is always the best approach. You may want to discuss these guidelines with your students to see if they are consistent with your students' experiences and to explore with them other behaviors that are appropriate in cross-cultural interactions.

- **Eye contact**
  Direct eye contact is not consistent with cultural norms for many African Americans and Hispanics.

- **Proximity**
  How close people stand when talking to each other varies from culture to culture.

- **Taking turns**
  Italian households often find family members talking at the same time and many African Americans show they are listening by jumping in to agree or disagree as others are speaking.

- **Touching**
  Some cultures are comfortable with physical contact being part of their communication style while others such as Middle Easterners, for example, might not find touching to be appropriate.

- **Loudness and Tempo**
  Speed of delivery, volume and degree of emotionality vary among cultures. Many people including some Native American societies value silence and contemplation and do not feel compelled to always respond during a conversation.

52

SHARE
to Show You Care

> *Caring is everything; Nothing matters but caring.*
>
> —The last words of Baron Friedrich Von Hugel

Purpose

The need for attention is often pointed to as the source of many childhood behaviors — especially inappropriate ones. So to give students an opportunity to receive attention, to be really listened to, contributes greatly to their sense of belonging.

The purpose of this activity is for students to develop effective listening skills. These skills will be practiced over and over again in the activities that follow.

Procedure

1.   Hand out the Share Worksheet and discuss these listening skills with your students. Ask students for examples and do some age-appropriate role plays to be sure that the guidelines are understood. For instance:

   - To demonstrate **S**: Be Still. Be Silent
     Have a student come up to the front of the room and tell you about one of his/her favorite movies. While the student is talking, interrupt with your comments about your own favorite movie.

- To demonstrate **R**: Restate
  This time have the student tell you about his/her favorite movie and at appropriate intervals, restate what the student has been saying to check for accuracy.

2.   Hand out copies of the Share The Wealth Worksheet.

3.   Describe the simulated situation to the students. The class has just received a donation of $100 from a wealthy member of the community. Their task is to decide how to spend the $100. The worksheet specifies the available options. Each team has 20 minutes to reach a consensus on how to spend the money. If they are unable to decide within that time–frame, the money will be given to another class instead.

4.   The team agreement is that before any student can state his or her point of view, he or she must restate the point made by the person who spoke just before him or her. The students are to SHARE—to show they care—following the guidelines for effective listening.

5.   Have each group select a moderator who will be in charge of making sure that everyone follows the agreements. This student will not otherwise get involved in the discussion.

6.   Give a two-minute warning before the end of the time period, and then call time at the end of the 20 minutes.

7.   Have someone from each team report on what option the group decided on and the process used to arrive at it.

8.   Engage the entire class in a discussion of effective listening skills and how they affect group process.

   - In what ways was it helpful?
   - Were there times when it got in the way?
   - How can these skills be applied in other areas of their lives?

---

*F*rom listening comes wisdom, and from speaking repentance.

— Italian Proverb

Share Worksheet
Effective Listening Skills

S   SHHHHHHHH!
BE **STILL**. BE **SILENT**.

H   HEAR WHAT THEY ARE SAYING.
HEAR WHAT THEY MEAN.

A   PAY **ATTENTION**. **ALLOW** THEM TO SPEAK.
ACCEPT WHAT THEY SAY AS TRUE FOR THEM.

R   RESTATE WHAT YOU HEARD THEM SAY TO BE SURE YOU GOT THE
MESSAGE.

E   ENCOURAGE THEM TO SPEAK.
MAKE IT EASY FOR THEM TO SAY WHAT THEY WANT.

One of the best ways to persuade others is with your ears —by listening to them.

— Dean Rusk

Share the Wealth Worksheet

Your class has received a $100 donation from a wealthy member of the community. As a group, you must decide on how to spend the money from among the options listed below.

You have 20 minutes to come to a decision, otherwise the money will be given to another class. Your group must all agree on the choice.

Options:

1.   Divide the money equally among all the class members.

2.   Use the money to pay for a field trip related to a class project.

3.   Give the money to the physical education department for more sports equipment.

4.   Use the money to buy toys for a program like Toys for Tots for children less fortunate than yourselves.

5.   Donate the money to an organization that provides meals for AIDS patients who are not well enough to care for themselves.

6.   Use the money to buy blankets and distribute them to people who are homeless.

7.   Use the money to set up a recycling program to help save the environment.

8.   Spend the money on a fun party for your class.

53

Are You Listening?

Listening is not the same as waiting to speak.

— Anonymous

Purpose

Students will practice strategies to improve their ability to listen actively and to notice nonverbal clues the reveal meaning.

Procedure

1. Demonstrate the difference between verbal and nonverbal communication by saying (in a sad voice):

    This is the happiest day of my life.

    (Then in a bored voice): *This is the most exciting thing that's ever happened to me.*

    Ask the students what was wrong with what was said. Elicit answer that you didn't say what you meant. Congratulate them for being good listeners because they heard the meaning behind the words.

2. Continue:

    If you were a detective, what clues could you spot to tell how people really feel despite what they say? These are nonverbal clues because they don't include the verbal part, or talking.

    Ask students to think about nonverbal clues they have seen or heard. List some of the following items:

    Voice: angry, hurt, sad, happy, excited, bored, etc.

Eyes: not focused on listener, making eye contact, darting.

Posture: straight, bent over, sitting sprawled out, sitting up rigidly, leaning towards the other person.

Gestures: nervous actions, hands all over face, arms tightly crossed.

Other: smiling face, wrinkled brow.

After the list has been compiled, have students dramatize some nonverbal clues as you did earlier.

3.   Next, say:

Now we're going to find out some ways that we can better understand people's verbal messages, what they're actually saying.

Note: *In some cultures (Asian, for example) it may be considered impolite to make eye contact.*

Select a very verbal student with good self-esteem. Tell that person privately that you're going to interrupt frequently, but that he or she should continue talking. Then have the student talk about any subject (a problem, a TV show, something that happened last night, feelings about something), while you interrupt frequently, demonstrating poor listening skills. Some common interruptions include:

— Turning the conversation to yourself. ("That reminds me of the time I . . . .")
— Giving unsolicited advice.
— Being sarcastic.
— Being unsympathetic. ("I don't know why you got so upset; everybody has a pet that dies. You'll get a new one.")

4.   Ask students to describe what you did that showed you were a poor listener. List their answers on the board and have them add other examples:

Poor listeners:

— Interrupt
— Think about what they want to say next.
— Turn the conversation to themselves.
— Try to solve the problem as if the speakers couldn't do it alone.

— Argue.
— Listen only to the words and not the feelings.
— Don't say anything and never react to the speakers.
— Are sarcastic.
— Ignore nonverbal clues.

5. Have students work in triads (groups of three — A, B, C). Student A is the first talker and can choose any subject to talk about (for example, what happened on the weekend); Student B will demonstrate poor listening skills; Student C is the observer who notes examples of poor listening skills. Have students trade roles after one minute, then trade again so that each person can experience all three roles. When the triads are finished, have students briefly report back interesting observations to the class.

6. Now ask the class to list examples of good listening. Restate the items in the above list in a positive mode and be sure to include the following:

— Use nonverbal positive responses: "uh-huh," nod head, move in closer.
— Paraphrase periodically to make sure you understand.
— Be nonjudgmental.

7. Have students in the same triad now talk to each other and demonstrate good listening skills, then briefly report back to class.

Note: *This activity can be repeated frequently. Be aware of cultural differences among students, such as varying needs for personal space.*

Follow-Up Activities

1. Have students listen at home, on the school playground, in the classroom, at the market, and so forth, for good and poor listeners and orally share examples of both to the class — no names please.

2. Have students give written examples of the good and poor listeners they see.

3. Make a class chart. Give a sticker each time someone demonstrates good listening.

4. Have students make posters with the themes "How To Be A Good Listener" or "How To Be A Poor Listener." Use cartoon-type characters — all ears, intelligent look — for the good listener, and a big mouth and impatient expression for the poor listener.

5 4

Name That Team

> *Culture is both an intellectual phenomenon and a moral one.*
>
> —Raisa M. Gorbachev

Purpose

This exercise is used to help students feel greater ownership for their team and a sense of identity with it.

Procedure

1. Remind students of what constitutes a culture (Activity 20) that it is a group's way of meeting their human needs by surviving in and adapting to their environment. Ask them to brainstorm with you the different aspects of a culture such as language, food, music, as well as values, beliefs, myths and so forth.

    Continue the discussion by explaining that businesses also use the term *culture* as in *corporate culture* to define itself. Corporate culture refers to the company's name, image, values, and ways of doing business.

    Next, refer to sports teams—both school or professional—that also try to create a culture with a name, an image or mascot, particular colors, sometimes a song or cheer. This is designed to build loyalty among both players and fans.

    Ask the students to identify their favorite teams and aspects of their culture. For example: Los Angeles Raiders (black and silver pirate logo); New Orleans Saints (gold and black—fleur de lis logo); Boston Celtics (green and white—leprechaun logo).

Let the students know that they are now going to create their own team culture.

2.   Invite the students to move into small groups.

3.   Tell them that as a team they are to agree on a name for their team. The name must be one that every one on the team feels good about.

4.   Remind them of their team agreements and ask them to use effective listening skills, SHARE, to be sure everyone is heard.

5.   Suggest that they follow these steps:

    a.   Discuss and agree on what positive characteristics of their team they want their name to convey. For example:

        "Bears" suggests strength
        "Cougars," speed
        "Giants," power

        One way to help students identify possible characteristics is to have them do the "If You Were...," Activity 9.

    b.   Brainstorm all the possible names that could be used to communicate this quality. Consider names that take into account the multicultural makeup of the group.

    c.   Discuss the advantages and disadvantages of each name and select the one that works best. Once again, everyone on the team must accept the name that is chosen.

    d.   Discuss how the "official" team name should look— printed or cursive, all caps on upper and lower case, and so forth—and where it can be used—book covers, T-shirts, next to students' names on class assignments, and so forth.

6.   When the teams are finished, have them each make a presentation to the rest of the class describing their team name and how they came to choose it.

7.   On subsequent days, use the same procedure to have Student Teams decide on:

    • Team Colors   • Team Song or Cheer
    • Team Logo or Mascot   • Team Motto
    • Team Handshake or Greeting

55

Team Trust Walk

You may be deceived if you trust too much, but you will live in torment unless you trust enough.

—Dr. Frank Crane

Purpose

Trust is an essential quality for being in a relationship or part of a community. This exercise is designed to increase students' ability to trust and be trusted. By trusting others, we empower each other and allow ourselves to become even more worthy of trust.

Materials

This activity can be done by having students shut their eyes or you can provide one blindfold (6 x 8-inch strip of cloth) for every student.

Procedure

1.   For this activity you will need to find a suitable area of the school. You will need a space large enough for the class to move around freely in teams without running into each other or other students. You also need some privacy from outsiders who might disrupt the activity. The space should have some variation in terrain—some slopes or stairs, different surfaces to walk on, and so on. However, it should not have any dangerous areas where students could be injured. Ideally the area would be open enough for you to observe the teams as they walk. If there is no one area large enough, delegate students to be stationed in each area so that they can monitor the activity. Ideal places are the playground, a gymnasium, or a quiet wing of the school building.

2. Have the students get into their teams. Let them know that they will be going on a "trust walk." Everyone on the team is blindfolded (or has his or her eyes closed) except the leader.

   Each student places his or her right hand on the right shoulder of the person in front. The student at the head of the line is the leader. He or she is not blindfolded and without talking leads the team on the walk. The leader seeks to make the walk fun and interesting, but not dangerous. The students lined up behind the leader get nonverbal cues from the movements of the person in front of them.

3. Before starting on the walk, discuss the risk factor and ask the students to communicate to their teammates any concerns they have.

4. Have the group make agreements that will allow the activity to be done safely.

5. Request that they make a serious commitment to each other to support their safety and well-being.

6. Once you reach the designated area, give the students their blindfolds. Ask them to decide who is going to be the leader. After five to seven minutes, call time and have the students remove their blindfolds. Give the teams a few minutes to talk about their experience of leading and being led. Then have the teams change leaders and continue the exercise.

7. After the second team's round of five to seven minutes, tell them to stop and remove their blindfolds. Once again, give them a few minutes to talk about their experiences. Have them acknowledge their teammates for guiding them and also for trusting them. Ask them to discuss the following questions: If you were going to do this activity again, what changes would you make? Suggest that they discuss answers to this question with their teammates.

8. Bring the class together in a circle for closure. Have them take turns sharing what it felt like to be blindfolded and also what it felt like to be the leader. Possible discussion questions:

   Did you feel fully comfortable and supported by your leader? If not, what could your leader have done differently to make you feel more trusting? What could you have done differently to make yourself feel more trusting of them?

   As the leader, how did it feel to have someone else depend on you? Did you feel worthy of the trust?

5 6

Team Problem Solving

***P**roblems are the price you pay for progress.*

—Branch Rickey

Purpose

When problems arise at school, it is often best to let students be part of the solution. This activity provides guidelines for arriving at win-win solutions through team problem solving.

Procedure

1. The concepts involved in this activity can be discussed with the class as a whole to set the stage for any particular problems that may arise.

2. Open the discussion in a manner similar to this: "What do all the following activities have in common?"

    football games
    baseball games
    all professional sports
    poker
    Old Maid
    all other card games (except solitaire)
    most game shows
    grading systems in schools (sometimes)
    court cases
    political elections
    war

    Let the students respond. If they get it, congratulate them. If not, say, "Each of these activities has winners and losers. The fact is, many activities in life are set up as win-lose situations. To be a winner, it seems you have to defeat someone else. However, if you look at what makes a winning team, you notice that not only do they work together for a common goal, but they also care about each other. As each member grows in strength and ability, the entire team becomes more powerful. What this means is that there are no losers on a winning team. When problems arise, they are everybody's business. Solutions are found that allow each and every member to benefit. (Remember the lesson about their being no excess puzzle pieces in Activity 29, "Everyone Belongs"?) You may be wondering if it is possible to have a game with no losers. Take a look and see."

3.   Brainstorm typical problems that arise at school or discuss an actual problem that needs to be addressed. For example:

   - Students in the playground got into a fight over which group would use the soccer ball.

   - One group of students were picking on another group, making negative racial comments.

   - On a cooperative learning science project, one of the students on the team is not doing his or her fair share of the work. So, either other teammates will have to do extra work or the whole team's grade will suffer.

4.   Distribute copies of the Team Problem Solving Worksheet and review this five-step process with the class.

5.   Now take one of the typical problems identified above or use the actual problem you want resolved, and practice using the five-steps to arrive at a solution.

6.   Next, have the students get into their teams and work through one of the other problems using the ABCDE guidelines on the worksheet.

7.   Have each team report on their process and solution to the problem.

8.   Indicate that this tool is available to them if problem situations arise in their own lives at school, at home, or at work.

Team Problem Solving Worksheet
Simple as ABCDE

A Agree on what the problem is.
  - What are the facts: Who, What, When, Where, How and Why?

B Brainstorm possible solutions.
  - What do all interested parties want and need?

C Choose the best solution.
  - How could everyone's needs best be served?

D Do it!
  - Who will do what by when?

E Evaluate and return to **A** if necessary.
  - Is it working?
  - Has the problem been solved?
  - What more needs to happen?

57

The Three Blind Men and the Elephant

> *N*othing that God ever made is the same thing to more than one person.
>
> —Zora Neale Hurston

Purpose

The purpose of this activity is for students to take greater ownership of their own viewpoint and to be more accepting of the points of view of others. It will help establish an important foundation for the next activity related to resolving conflicts.

Materials

Any object that has two different sides, such as a book that has a photograph on the front cover and a blank back cover, a t-shirt with an image on one side and nothing on the other, and so forth.

Procedure

1. Read the following story* to your students.

   Many years ago, there was a village where all of the citizens were blind. The older people told their children frightening stories about a monster who lived in the forest just outside of the village. Most people were afraid to enter the forest, for fear of being attacked by the ferocious beast.

---

* This familiar story is adapted from *World Tales* by Idries Shah (New York: Harcourt Brace Jovanovich, 1979).

One day, three leaders of the city decided to go into the forest together and find out whether the stories were true. Together they ventured out, and eventually they located an elephant, who was grazing contentedly in a meadow.

Now, the three men were blind, so they couldn't see the "monster." One of the blind men reached out and grasped the elephant's ear. Another groped around and felt the elephant's trunk. And the third took hold of one of the elephant's feet and legs. Armed with this information about the creature, they went back home.

When they returned to the village, the three men called all the villagers around them. The townspeople were eager to hear a description of the creature that had inspired such fear. The first man, who had felt the elephant's ear, said, "I laid my hands on the creature, and I can tell you what it is. It is a large, rough thing, wide and broad, like a rug."

The second man, who had felt the elephant's trunk, broke in. "No," he cried, "I laid my hands on the creature, and I can tell you what it is. It is like a straight and hollow pipe, awful and destructive."

Then the third man, who touched the feet and legs, "Both of you are wrong. I laid my hands on the creature, and I can tell you what it is. It is mighty and firm like a pillar."

2. Now, stand in the middle of the class and hold up an object that has two different sides.

3. Ask one student who is sitting in a position to see only one side to describe what he or she sees.

4. Then ask a student who can only see the other side of the object to describe what it looks like from his or her viewpoint.

5. Repeat what each of the two students answered and ask the class who is right. When the students respond that both points of view are correct, ask how this is possible.

6. Explain that usually when people see things from different points of view, they assume that their perspective is right and therefore the other person must be wrong. This is the source of much conflict and fighting in the world. This demonstration makes it clear that it is possible for different people to have different points of view and that these can not only co-exist but also enhance each person's total understanding of the situation.

7. This would serve as an excellent introduction to a multicultural lesson or discussion. You could select an historical event and consider it from various viewpoints. For example, what was the

first Thanksgiving like for the children of the Pilgrims and the Native Americans?

The Civil War takes on an interesting perspective when viewed from the 186,000 African Americans who served — a third of whom died — in the Union Army.

It would be fascinating to consider what the California Gold Rush must have been like for the Chinese migrants who joined the "Forty-Niners."

An excellent reference source is Ronald Takaki's *A Different Mirror: A History of Multicultural America* (Boston: Little, Brown. 1993).

8.   This activity could also be used to help students understand how they can deal with their own personal conflicts in a nonviolent manner. The next exercise provides a structure for conflict management.

58

Taking A Stand

> *Truth arises from disagreement amongst friends.*
>
> —David Hume

Background

This activity distinguishes between assertive, passive, and aggressive behavior.

Assertive behavior: States ideas, opinions, feelings, and needs positively and confidently. Stands up for own rights without violating the rights of others. Qualities include being open, direct, and honest. Behavior is appropriate to the situation.

Passive behavior: Opposite of assertive behavior. Does not state ideas, opinions, or needs openly, directly, or honestly. Avoids any confrontation.

Aggressive behavior: Focuses on own message without concern for the rights of others. Behaviors include harshness, sarcasm, hostility.

Purpose

To encourage students to exhibit assertive rather than passive or aggressive behavior.

Procedure

1.   At the start of the lesson say:

    Today we are going to learn about three kinds of behavior: assertive, passive, and aggressive. Please watch.

2.   Sit at a student desk in front of the room. (Before beginning this scene, select one student and rehearse him or her to grab a pencil out of your hand.) React aggressively: immediately get up and threaten the student, look furious, raise voice, and so forth. Write the word "aggressive" on the board.

3.   Replay the scene. This time react passively: look around fearfully and say in a stage whisper as if thinking aloud, "I hope the teacher saw that. I don't like sitting here. I'll tell the teacher after school. I hope she'll change my seat." Write the word "passive" on the board.

4.   Replay the scene a third time. React assertively and say, "It makes me angry when you grab my pencil because I can't concentrate on my work. I want you to stop doing that. The next time you need to use my eraser, just ask me." Write the word "assertive" on the board.

Note: *If you don't enjoy acting out these vignettes, two students can be trained before the lesson to enact the scenes.*

5.   Based on the above scenes, have students discuss the characteristics of the three types:

	AGGRESSIVE	**PASSIVE**	**ASSERTIVE**
Voice:	Harsh, loud, coarse	Timid, breathy	Strong, clear
Face:	Angry, cold	Fearful, pinched	Open, relaxed
Body Language:	Ready to fight	Defensive, bent over	Relaxed, straight
Attitude:	"You're wrong!"	"I don't want to make trouble."	"I stand up for my rights without hurting others."

6.   Explain the following five tools for assertion. After each explanation, have students role-play each tool. Elicit stories of real situations that have happened to class members. Ask them to think of the times when they wished they had spoken up but didn't know how to or got into a fight and now wish they could have prevented it.

  a. Be straightforward: Give a clear message telling others what you want.

  b. "I" message: It has three parts. First, say how you feel (frustrated, angry, irritated). Then describe the behavior of the other person that's making you feel that way. End with the consequences to you as a result. "I feel angry when you keep talking during class and I can't concentrate on what the teacher is saying."

  c. Broken record: Keep repeating the same message. Do not get involved in any other issue, so that you don't get sidetracked: "Don't take my pencil again."

  d. Fogging: When someone is critical of your behavior, agree with any truths or feelings the other person has and make no commitment to change your behavior. This technique is very useful when people are complaining about you. Often when you discuss a complaint, someone has to be right and someone has to be wrong. Some examples of fogging: "I understand that you're mad" and "You may be right."

  e. Nonverbal: Practice speaking in a clear, powerful voice. Stand straight. Make eye contact.

7. Give class a situation: "A friend keeps copying from your paper and you don't like it." Have class come up with three responses: aggressive, passive, and assertive. Then break class into small groups and let each group devise problems and three responses to these problems. Have groups share their results with the entire class.

8. Role-play problem situations which occur often in your class, making sure there is an emphasis on the assertive responses.

59

Win - Win

> **W**e are visitors on this planet. We are here for ninety, a hundred years at the very most. During that period we must try to do something good, something useful with our lives. Try to be at peace with yourself and help others share that peace. If you contribute to other people's happiness, you will find the true goal, the true meaning of life.
>
> —The Dalai Lama

Purpose

For students to understand the meaning of win-win negotiation and be able to apply these principles to their own experience.

Procedure

1. Introduce the lesson by saying:

    When you are in an argument with someone and that person acts as if he or she always has to win over you, how do you feel?

    (Possible answers: angry, frustrated, mad, want to give up.)

    What happens when you are the person who always has to win? How do you think the other person feels?

    Probably like a loser. When you have to win, the other person loses.

    Today we're going to learn about a different way to get what you want where both sides win. It's called "win-win negotiation." You will learn how to get what you want without making an enemy of your opponent.

2. Present the following situation to the class:

The upper grade students at Blaine School are assigned play areas at recess time. They want the principal to change the rules so they can have free play areas. How can they persuade the principal to make the change? Before you try to resolve the problem, let's look at some steps to win-win negotiation.

3.   Prepare chart of principles of win-win negotiation or list them on the chalkboard. Ask students to give an example of each principle based on the play-area situation in Procedure 2 above.

4.   Divide class into cooperative learning groups. Have them discuss the play-area situation and enact the scene with the principal and students negotiating. Then have each group act out its scene for the class. If this situation is too difficult or meaningless to your class, make up an appropriate situation. For example: The class would like to cook but the teacher feels it is too expensive and too messy.

Using the seven steps of win-win negotiation, how can the students persuade the teacher to allow cooking?

5.   Briefly discuss how each group demonstrated one or more of the principles of win-win negotiation.

6.   Leave the chart on principles of win-win negotiation on the wall until students have mastered it. Refer to it often when you see a student using any of the principles or when a problem comes up.

7.   Have students identify a problem and use the worksheets on the following two pages as a guide for creating a win-win solution.

Follow-Up Activities

1.   Assign to cooperative learning groups another negotiation situation: for example, between parent and child, between teacher and student, between friend and friend, between student and sibling. Have group go through steps in discussion and then enact negotiation for class.

2.   Look for a real-life opportunity to use the system with the class.

3.   Optional assignment: If student has a situation at home or at school that is right for win-win negotiation, have student write it up and present it to class.

Seven Steps For Win-Win Negotiation

1. Know what you want (free play areas).

2. Know what the other person wants (a peaceful playground with no fighting).

3. Know what the other person's objections might be (too much fighting if people don't have an assigned place to go).

4. Know what you both agree on. (Both sides want students to enjoy their recess time.)

5. Stick to the issue. (Just talk about the play areas; don't get involved with homework policies, the lunch program, whether the principal is fair or not, and so forth.)

6. Think of other options in case original request is denied. (Try out free play one day a week, have area captains in charge of play areas, and so forth.)

7. Begin negotiating. Focus on both sides winning so no one has to lose.

Name_____   Date_____

Seven Steps for Win-Win Negotiation Worksheet

Problem_____

_____

_____

1. Know what you want._____

   _____

2. Know what the other person wants._____

   _____

3. Know what the other person's objections might be._____

   _____

4. Know what you both agree on._____

   _____

5. Stick to the issue._____

   _____

6. Think of other options in case original request is denied._____

   _____

   _____

7. Begin negotiating. Focus on both sides winning so no one has to lose.

   _____

   _____

60

Fighting Fair, Part I

> *The world is wide, and I will not waste my life in friction when it could be turned into momentum.*
>
> —Frances Willard

Purpose

Students will learn to create rules for solving conflicts.

Procedure

1. To get the discussion started, ask the class:

    Remember the last time we had a problem on the playground? Here are some of the things that happened to stop you from solving the problem.

2. Show students the following pre-made chart:

    ### FIGHTING FOULS

    1. Name calling
    2. Blaming
    3. Not listening
    4. Getting even
    5. Bringing up the past
    6. Threats
    7. Pushing and hitting
    8. Bossing
    9. Put-downs

3. Discuss each item briefly with class.

4. Put class into cooperative groups and read the short script that follows:

FIGHTING FAIR

Characters: Tammy, Anna, Michelle, Rocky, Mario, and the Coach

(The girls arrive at the volleyball court.)

Tammy: We need to practice for the game tomorrow with Mrs. Ford's class.

Anna: Yea! Look, Rocky and Mario are still here. Hey, Mario!

Mario: We're busy. Don't interrupt!

Michelle: We want to play. When will you be done?

Rocky: Get lost! We're using this court. You girls don't even know how to play.

Michelle: You've had it all morning!

Mario: And we still do, stupid! So get out or I'll get you out!

(The boys and girls start threatening, name-calling, and pushing. Coach enters.)

Coach: What's the problem here?

Rocky: The girls butted into our game.

Tammy: We just want to use the court.

Mario: We were here first!

Coach: Do you want to solve this, or stay angry?

5. Each group writes its own ending without using any Fighting Fouls.

6. Each group presents its ending to the class.

7. Chart techniques used to solve problems. Chart could be called "Fighting Fair" and may include:

FIGHTING FAIR

1. Identify the problem.
2. Focus on the problem.
3. Attack the problem, not the person.
4. Listen with an open mind.
5. Treat a person's feelings with respect.
6. Take responsibility for your own actions.

8.   Post final "Fighting Fouls" and "Fighting Fair" charts.

61

Fighting Fair, Part II:

Game Plan

> *L*ove is not a doctrine. Peace is not an international agreement. Love and Peace are beings who live as possibilities in us.
>
> —Mary Caroline Richards

Purpose

To have students make an agreement to follow rules of Fighting Fair in solving problems between themselves.

Procedure

1.   Build on the previous lesson by saying:

     Have you ever had a problem with someone that you really wanted to solve, but couldn't? You tried everything you could think of, but you just ended up in a bigger fight. This can happen to anybody. People who learn to fight fairly can solve their problems and gain the respect and friendship of the other person. Today we will set up rules, and all of us will make an agreement to follow these rules of fighting fairly.

2.   Have a student reread the lists of "Fighting Fouls" and "Fighting Fair."

3.   Write on the board the following:

GAME PLAN FOR FIGHTING FAIR

1. Take only two minutes each to state problem and feelings.

2. State what you prefer and what you will do differently next time.

3. Shake hands after the problem is resolved.

4. Explain each section of the game plan.

   a. Each person has two minutes or less to state the problem. Only what happened and feelings about it can be said. He or she should stand in front of the class and face the other person eye to eye. No one else can talk during these two minutes.

   b. After each person has had two minutes, the first person says what he or she prefers the other person to do next time and what he or she will do differently next time.

      Example:

      Next time, please do not push me off the bench. It embarrasses me. Just tell me you want your seat back. Next time, I will move over quickly and make a place for you.

   c. Both students shake hands. (The class can make its own special handshake.) The handshake shows that two people who had a problem have solved it by fighting fairly.

5. Ask the class if there are any questions or comments. Then, have the whole class stand up in agreement with the "Game Plan for Fighting Fair." Have students shake hands all around, using the class's new special handshake.

6. Remind students to use the game plan the next time a problem arises. Have a game plan up on the wall, readily available along with the lists of "Fighting Fouls" and "Fighting Fair."

62

Fighting Fair, Part III:

Practice the Game Plan

> *It seems to me that there are two great enemies of peace — fear and selfishness.*
>
> —Katherine Paterson

Purpose

This final activity in the sequence will give students practice in using the rules of "Fighting Fair."

Procedure

1. After the rules of "Fighting Fair" and specific rules for resolving classroom conflicts have been discussed and explained, begin with a story about students in a conflict. (See sample problems below for additional conflict situations.)

    Let's say that Michael is writing and Anna thinks the pencil he is using belongs to her. Anna tells Michael, "Give me my pencil!" Michael answers, "It's mine!" What could Anna and Michael do to solve this?

2. Ask students for suggestions.

3. *Now let's have two students pretend they are Anna and Michael, and practice our rules for "Fighting Fair."*

4. Choose two volunteers to act out what they would say following "Fighting Fair" rules. Classmates may call out fouls when they hear them.

5. Have students suggest things that could have been done differently.

6. Put students in pairs and ask each pair to select a problem. Then have each pair role-play the problem and its resolution in front of the class according to the "Game Plan for Fighting Fair" on pages 233-234.

Sample Problems:

1. Tran and Sara are playing with the class football. Sal and Marion would like to play and ask if they can. Tran and Sara say, "No." What should Sal and Marion do?

2. Martha is very angry because she came outside late and her friends are all playing a game. The teams are even and her friend says, "You can't play because the teams are even." So Martha runs through the middle of the game and disrupts it. What can they do?

3. Carl found a drawing on the floor and ripped it up. Christina found the pieces in the wastebasket and said, "Who stole my drawing and threw it away?" Another classmate said it was Carl. What should they say?

Follow-Up Activities

1. The next time a real problem comes up between two students, stop the class and have them come to the center of the class. Ask all children to stop the ongoing activity and face the two students. Then have the two students follow the "Game Plan for Fighting Fair" and solve the problem in front of the whole class. If one of the students commits a foul, the classmates should raise their hands and call it out.

2. Whenever a problem arises between two students, give them five minutes privately in a corner to work it out using the "Game Plan." If it goes past five minutes or they cannot solve it by themselves, have them come to the center of the class and follow the above activity. Be sure to tell the class that the "Game Plan" will be used in the future whenever it is needed.

63

The Meaning of Gangs

I know you cannot hate other people without hating yourself.

—Oprah Winfrey

Purpose

The purpose of this series of activities on gangs is to help students make wise choices about membership in certain groups. In this first lesson, students will learn what the word "gang" means, describe neighborhood gangs, and discuss possible good and bad aspects of gang membership.

Procedure

1.   Ask the class:

What does the word "gang" mean to you?

Class responds.

2.   Then explain:

The word "gang" originally meant a group of people who are close.

3.   Hold a class discussion. Ask students to describe gangs in their neighborhoods (if any) and the things that gang members have in common (behavior, dress, posture, symbols, signals).

4.   Record students' comments on chart paper or on the chalkboard.

   Options: (a)   make one long list

        (b)   With students' help, classify characteristics of gangs as positive or negative.

5.   Hold a class discussion on positive aspects of gangs and groups. For example:

    a.   Being in a gang makes you feel like you belong. (Wanting to belong is normal.)

    b.   Being in a gang makes you feel special.

    c.   You can do good things for your neighborhood in a group.

6.   Continue the discussion by examining the negative aspects of gangs and groups. For example:

    a.   Some people do things they think are wrong in order to belong.

    b.   Sometimes gang members do things that change the neighborhood in a negative way, such as fighting, stealing, taking drugs, graffiti, acts of violence and vandalism.

Note: For additional resources for dealing with youth violence, contact:

- *The Joseph Matteucci Foundation for Youth Non-Violence offers training for young people to participate and run their own violence-mediation programs in schools. (510) 889-7451; www.jmf4peace.org*

- *Teens, Crime and the Community, created by the National Crime Prevention Council, provides a learning kit and strategies for crime prevention in neighborhoods. (202) 261-4161; www.nationaltcc.org*

- *Center for the Prevention of School Violence offers monthly violence-prevention lesson plans for elementary school teachers and parents. (800) 299-6054; www.ncsu.edu/cpsv/*

64

Some Facts About Gangs

> *O*nly ways you can keep folks hating is to keep them apart and separated from each other.
>
> —Margaret Walker

Purpose

The students will become aware of facts and opinions about gangs and gang activity.

Procedure

1. Introduce the activity by saying:

    I am going to give you a short quiz to see what you know and think about gangs. Some of the questions have a correct answer, and others are a matter of opinion. All you have to do is answer true or false on your paper.

2. Hand out the quiz on page 241 and ask students to take it in silence.

3. After students have taken the quiz, use their answers as springboards for discussion.

4. Discuss one issue at a time. Some hints for discussion are:

    a. *In the past many gangs were Caucasian or Anglo. They were often composed of one neighborhood or ethnic group, such as Italian or Jewish. Today, there are gangs of every race and color. Do you know any gangs in which people of different races are members?*

    b. *Many gangs in the past were originally formed as clubs and did not participate in any criminal or illegal (against the law) activities. Do you know any things that gang members do together that are legal and positive (worthwhile)?*

c. *It is very difficult to get out of a gang once you have joined. It is easier not to join in the first place. However, there are counselors who have been trained to help people get out of gangs. They have helped many people and usually can be found at a neighborhood youth center or other helpful groups. What youth centers or other helpful groups are in your neighborhood?*

d. *Although many people who live near gang members fear and respect them, most people in the country do not respect them. It may be very hard to get a good job if the employer knows you have been in a gang. What is the difference between fear and respect? Give examples. Why would someone not want to hire an ex-gang member?*

e. *It is possible to remove a tattoo, but it is expensive, painful, and difficult. Do you think an employer would hesitate to hire someone who has a tattoo? Why?*

f. *Graffiti, like gang names or signs, is used to glorify gangs and mark their turf or territory, and can cause fights. How do you think graffiti looks on walls, murals, and buildings?*

Quiz

Answer "T" for true, "F" for false.

_____ 1. All gang members are either black or Latino. (or Filipino, Vietnamese, and so forth, depending on the area in which you live)

_____ 2. Gangs have always been violent.

_____ 3. Once you join a gang it is easy to quit if you want to.

_____ 4. Most people have a lot of respect for gang members.

_____ 5. It is easy to remove a tattoo if you don't want it any more.

_____ 6. Graffiti is used by gang members because it looks nice.

65

Saying No, Part I

> *B*elieving in our students' resilience requires foremost that we believe in our own innate capacity to transform and change.
>
> —Bonnie Benard

Purpose

Students will practice ways of resisting pressure to join gangs that participate in illegal activities.

Procedure

1. Begin by saying:

    Have you ever been forced or pressured by another student or an older person into doing something you knew was wrong? (Pause.) *Tell us about it.* (Allow time for sharing.)

2. After student responses, continue by saying:

    At your age you are just learning about the grown-up world and experimenting with things that are part of growing up. Sometimes you want to experiment with things that are forbidden or risky.

    We all feel unhappy sometimes, and growing up can be difficult. It's normal to want to take risks and try new things. It is important, though, to realize the differences between reasonable, safe risks and dangerous risks. Sometimes we have to follow rules that we disagree with and deal with people who treat us poorly.

    We want to fit in, and we need other people to like us. Loneliness can be hard to handle. Often, friends and relatives will put a lot of pressure on us to do what they are doing. We have to think about what could happen if we go along with the crowd and then make up our minds about what to do. When our friends pressure us to do something, saying no can be hard. Sometimes going against what they want will make them angry. But we don't have to do everything our friends do in order to remain friends. Most people admire others who make up their own minds and stand up for themselves. If others don't like you because you won't go along with them about using drugs or getting into a gang, are they your real friends? Your real friends are those who want you to be your best.

Older friends who want you to join in a gang activity or do something for them are not doing it because they like you. They are probably doing it because they need you to do things they don't want to do, their dirty work. Is it worth the risks?

Every day we have to make big and little decisions. When you are unsure of what to do, talk to someone you trust—your parents, another adult who cares, or a friend who is not involved in gang or drug activities. Then make up your mind.

When people pressure you they are saying 'Don't think for yourself.' When you do think about the facts and the risks of a decision, saying no will be easier. Think about the bad things that could happen if you say yes and are caught doing something against the law. Saying no only takes one good reason.

3.   Now ask:

What are some of the things that can be done to resist pressure?

Pause to allow students time to give their ideas.

Now I'm going to tell you some more things you can do when you are under pressure.

    a. *Stand your ground — say no to anything you don't think is good for you. Keep it simple.*

    b. *Get away to where you are alone or with friends or family. Think about where you are in control.*

    c. *Be calm, even if you are scared inside. You will make better choices if you give yourself time to think and relax.*

    d. *Don't think it's easy to say yes, then change your mind. If you say yes, you are considered an easy target, and they will try again to convince you of whatever it was.*

> e. *Stay away from places where people use drugs or do things that are against the law.*

4. Make a poster of these ideas or write them on a paper and give copies to all students.

Follow-Up Activities

1. Ask students to make posters of different ways to resist pressure.

2. Have students practice making positive affirmations. For example:

   — I am in charge of my life.
   — I am in control of my thinking.
   — I can say no.
   — I respect myself and others.

66

Saying No, Part II

> *C*ourage is mastery of fear — not absence of fear.
>
> —Mark Twain

Purpose

Students will be able to say no to things that might harm their health and their relationships with others.

Procedure

1.   Ask students to repeat some of the negative effects of gang activities on their health (from smoking cigarettes, drug and alcohol abuse, injuries, antisocial behavior) and on their relationships (with family, friends, the community) and on their future (with jobs, the law).

2.   Explain that the students will help themselves stay out of trouble by learning to say no in real-life situations to things that might affect their health, relationships, or future.

3.   Split class into small groups of three to five students each.

4.   Give each group a card with a written description (see below) of a situation which they must develop and act out as a skit.

5.   Circulate among groups discussing and clarifying each situation and giving support.

6.   Ask groups to perform their skits. After each skit, ask for comments from the class on what group members said or did that was effective and what they could have done differently.

7.   Repeat that a person has the right to say no.

Sample situations for skit cards:

1.   Characters: Daniel, his younger sister, his father, his friend Al

       Situation: Daniel's father want him to stay home and do his homework. His friend wants him to go out with the members of the gang, who are planning a party with alcohol. His younger sister is your age. What does she say to Daniel?

2.   Characters: Juan, Joseph, and Tim

       Situation: The three boys are playing on a roof. Juan dares Joseph to jump off even though it is a dangerous jump. What should Tim and Joseph say?

3.   Characters: Mary, Tina, and Jena

       Situation: Jena has made $3 baby-sitting and has promised it to her little sister. Meanwhile, Tina and Mary ask Jena to give them the money to help them buy some drugs. What should Jena say to her friends?

4.   Characters: Kim, Lee, and Robert

       Situation: Kim and Lee have seen their friend Robert in the park talking to gang members in the neighborhood. Kim and Lee are worried about Robert. What should they do? Who could they talk to?

5.   Characters: Jack, David, and Gerry

       Situation: Jack, David, and Gerry are good friends. One day in the store David tells Gerry to take something without paying for it. Gerry is not sure what to do. Jack says, "Don't be chicken! Go ahead." What should Gerry do?

6 7

Making a Difference:

Creating Alternatives to Gang Membership

> **Y**ou must be the change you wish to see in the world.
>
> —Mahatma Gandhi

Purpose

Students will work together toward creating new after-school activity groups at their school.

Procedure

1. Open the activity with:

   We've been discussing what other groups students belong to.

   With the help of the students, make a list of groups students would like to belong to even if they do not exist at their school or in their neighborhood. Some examples might include: Boy Scouts, Girl Scouts, Little League, basketball teams, arts and crafts club, photography club, drill team, dance groups, and so forth.

2. Decide with the students which group they would like to establish at their school or in their neighborhood. Some groups may already exist at the school but the class may want others (such as a Cub Scout troop).

3. When students have decided on a goal (such as establishment of a scout group, have them brainstorm about the things they will need, such as a room at school, a leader, supplies, money).

4. Then have the class brainstorm how they can go about reaching their goal. (The class may need help in suggesting and developing ideas.) Some steps students may take in reaching their goals are:

   a. Circulating petitions. This is a great first step because it gets all students involved and excited.

   b. Writing letters specifying what students want, why they want it, and how the person or group they are writing to can help them.

      The class can contact the following people and groups:

      — Principal and Assistant Principal
      — Region Superintendent
      — Parents
      — Neighborhood businesses
      — Board of Education
      — Mayor
      — City Council
      — Newspapers
      — Parks and Recreation Department

      Letters may be written in groups or by individual students.

      Letters to parents may be photocopied and sent home.

5. Students may decide to have fund-raisers, such as a popcorn sale at recess. They may also decide to solicit funds from large organizations.

6. If the class can actually create a new group in their school or their neighborhood, they will learn one of the most valuable lessons you can give students: they can effect a change working through the system. They can make a difference. It is very important that you believe in the goal and work with the students.

Note: If creating a new group at the school seems unrealistic, start with a smaller goal, such as obtaining more playground equipment so students have more choices on the playground. Then work on a bigger goal with the next class, as confidence develops.

68

Let There Be Peace on Earth:

Conflict Management

> **W**e have grasped the mystery of the atom, and rejected the Sermon on the Mount. . . .The world has achieved brilliance without conscience. Ours is a world of nuclear giants and ethical infants. We know more about war than we do about peace, more about killing than we know about living.
>
> —General Omar Bradley

> **P**eople who fight fire with fire usually end up with ashes.
>
> —Abigail Van Buren

Purpose

In situations where the students who are involved in a conflict are unable to resolve it themselves, this activity will let them get assistance from their team.

---

* Adapted with permission from *Training High School Conflict Managers*. 1986, 1996. Published by Community Boards, San Francisco, CA. (415) 552-1250

Procedure

1. The steps in the conflict management process are outlined on the following pages. Review these with your students first.

2. Then set up a series of demonstration role-plays involving two students in conflict and four students serving as conflict managers. Start with simple conflicts before engaging in more difficult issues. You may use one of these sample problem situations or decide on others:

   • Students in the playground got into a fight over which group would use the soccer ball.

   • One group of students was picking on another group, making negative racial comments.

   • On a cooperative learning science project, one of the students on the team is not doing his or her fair share of the work. So, either other teammates will have to do extra work or the whole team's grade will suffer.

3. Introduce the students to the process, step by step, allowing for any questions and observations as you go along.

4. Next, divide the class into their teams and let them decide which two students will role-play the people who are in conflict and who will serve as conflict managers.

5. Select which conflict to use and have all groups working on the same one. Again, start with a simple conflict. Let them know that you are available as a resource if they need help.

6. When the groups are finished, bring them together for a class discussion. Find out how each group resolved the issue. Discuss the value of the process and how it can be used to resolve conflicts in the class, at school, at home, and in the community.

7. Continue with these small group role-plays over a period of days or weeks until everyone has had a turn and the skills of conflict management have been practiced to the point that students have integrated them. Gradually increase the severity of the conflict so that students are able to build upon earlier successes in applying conflict resolution skills to real life situations.

Conflict Management Worksheet

STEP 1   MEET SEPARATELY

- Conflict Managers meet separately with each person involved in the conflict.

- Introduce yourself.

- Describe the process and your role as conflict manager.

  The purpose of this process is to help you resolve the conflict. The way it works is, first you will tell me what happened from your point of view. While we are doing this, the other person involved in this conflict is describing his or her perception of what happened to another conflict manager.

  Then we will bring you both together and let you tell each other your side of the story, including your feelings about what happened. Once you understand each other's points of view better, we will explore possible solutions on which both of you can agree.

  My role is to facilitate communication and to help you two settle this issue.

- Explain the agreements.

  For this process to work, you must agree to the following:
  1. *You are willing to use this process to resolve the conflict.*
  2. *You will use appropriate language (no cursing or swearing).*
  3. *You will behave appropriately (no threat of violence).*
  4. *Everything that is said is confidential.*
  5. *Conflict managers must report cases involving child abuse, pregnancy, and threats of serious violence.*

- Get their agreement to cooperate.

  Do you agree to resolve the conflict by working with me through these five steps and by keeping these agreements?

- Ask the person now to explain what happened from his or her perspective to cause the conflict.

STEP 2   **MEET TOGETHER**

- Bring the two parties together and review what you said to each of the parties separately. Confirm that each has agreed to resolve the conflict through this process.

- Explain that during this first part each person will have a chance to talk about the situation without interruption. He or she is to speak directly to you as the conflict manager while the other person who is involved in the conflict gets to listen.

- Determine who will speak first, and ask this person to explain what happened from his or her perspective.

- Use effective listening skills (SHARE) to help clarify everyone's understanding of this person's experience.

- Summarize what you've heard, and confirm for accuracy.

- Acknowledge and validate: *Thank you very much for describing your experience of this conflict. Given your perspective, I can appreciate how you feel.*

- Repeat this part of the process with the other person involved in the dispute.

- Summarize both points of view, emphasizing similarities.

STEP 3   **BUILD MUTUAL UNDERSTANDING**

- Determine who will speak first, and have this person communicate directly to the other person involved.

- Encourage this person to communicate responsibly, using "I" messages. (How *I* felt rather than what *you* did.)

- Allow feelings and emotions to be expressed.

- Ensure understanding, by having the other person restate what he or she heard.

- Summarize, validate, and acknowledge.

STEP 4   **RESOLVE THE CONFLICT**

- Ask each person how he or she would like to see the situation resolved.

- Explore possible solutions that would work for both of them.

- Decide on a solution that is:
  —specific
  —realistic
  —mutually satisfactory.

- Schedule a follow-up session to take place within a week.

- Have each person sign an agreement to implement the solution and to be at the follow-up session.

- Acknowledge their willingness to resolve this issue.

STEP 5   FOLLOW-UP ON RESULTS

- Welcome everyone back.

- Review the purpose of this meeting and the issues involved in the conflict management process.

- Ask each person to share what has happened since the last session.

- Invite them to discuss what they learned through this process.

- If the issue has been resolved, acknowledge their success.

- If the issue remains unresolved, discover what didn't work and repeat steps in the conflict management process until a new commitment is made.

> *I want you to feel like loving your opponent, and the way to do it is to give them the same credit for honesty of purpose which you would claim for yourself.*
>
> —Mohandas Gandhi

69

Unequal Resources

> *In the beginning, our Creator gave all the races of mankind the same songs and the same drums to keep in touch with Him, to keep the faith. But people kept forgetting. In the fullness of time, the spiritual traditions of all the peoples—they are all the same—will be united again in a great gathering of their secret leaders. And they will gain power to remake the world.*
>
> —Mohawk prophecy as told by Tom Porter

Purpose

By now your students should be feeling comfortable within their teams. This activity will challenge them to be concerned with others who are outside their own group.

As a model of the world where some groups have more resources—money, power, and so forth—than others, students will explore the human bias for competing rather than cooperating.

Materials

Scissors, ruler, paper clips, glue, black felt tip markers and construction paper in six colors

Unequal Resources Task Sheet* for each group

Large envelopes to hold each group's resources. In the example below, the envelopes will contain the following resources as designated by group:

---

* Used with permission from J. William Pfeiffer and John E. Jones, *The 1972 Annual Handbook for Group Facilitators.* San Diego: University Associates, 1972.

Group I: Scissors, ruler, paper clips, pencils, and two 4" squares of red paper and two of white

Group II: Scissors, glue and 8 1/2" x 11" sheets of paper (two blue, two white, two gold)

Group III: Felt-tipped markers and 8 1/2" x 11" sheets of paper (two green, two white, two gold)

Group IV: 8 1/2" x 11" sheets of paper (one each: green, gold, blue, red and purple)

Procedure

1. Ask the students to get into their teams and be seated at their individual tables. Distribute an envelope of materials and a Tasks Sheet to each group.

2. Tell the groups not to open their materials until you tell them to begin the task. Then explain that each group has different materials but that each group must complete the same tasks. Explain that they may bargain for the use of the materials and tools in any way that is mutually agreeable. Emphasize that the first group to complete all tasks is the winner.

3. Give the signal to begin and observe as much group process and bargaining behavior as you can, so that you can supply feedback later.

4. Stop the process when one or more of the teams have accurately completed the items described on the task sheet.

5. Complete the activity with a discussion of the process by asking for observations concerning allocation of resources, use of resources, teamwork within groups, willingness of people to share with other groups, bargaining efforts, tendencies to compete rather than cooperate, and so forth.

6. Draw analogies between this experiment and the experience of minority groups and people in underdeveloped nations. Enlist student suggestions for how the world could be made to work better.

Note: *You may alter the complexity of the tasks and distribution of resources to fit the size of your class and age level of your students.*

Unequal Resources Tasks Sheet

Each group is to complete the following tasks:

1. Make a 3" by 3" square of white paper.

2. Make a 4" by 2" rectangle of gold paper.

3. Make a four–link paper chain, each link in a different color.

4. Make a T-shaped piece 3" by 5" in green and white paper.

5. Make a 4" by 4" flag, in any three colors.

The first group to complete all tasks is the winner. Groups may bargain with other groups for the use of materials and tools to complete the tasks on any mutually agreeable basis.

70

Streamers

> **O**ne joy scatters a hundred griefs.
>
> —Chinese Proverb

Purpose

The final activity in this section is meant to bring a sense of joy and celebration to the class as students thank one another for the positive ways in which everyone contributed.

Materials

Balls of yarn or crepe paper streamers, one roll per team; a different color for each team, preferably a color that is consistent with that team's colors.

Procedure

1. In order to have the students form a Circle of Friends that alternates members of each of the teams, have the students within each team count from one to five. Ask all the "ones" to sit beside each other in the full circle followed by the "twos," "threes," and so forth.

2. Let the students know that they are to say thank you to one of their teammates sitting in another part of the circle.

    They should be specific about what the other student did for which he or she is being thanked. For example:

    "Thank you for helping me understand the math assignment."

    "Thank you for calling me at home to find out how I was feeling the time I was absent."

"I appreciate your sense of humor."

3.   Give all the number "threes" a different color roll of crepe paper or ball of yarn. (See if you can match their team colors.) Instruct them to hold one end and gently toss the roll to the teammate that they are acknowledging.

4.   After all the "threes" have said their thank you's and tossed their streamers, the students holding the rolls go next in the same order as the rolls were received. Once again they hold onto their part and toss the rest of the roll to the student they are acknowledging.

Students should be told to pick students who have not yet been thanked and who are not holding a streamer.

5.   Continue the process until everyone has said thank you and been thanked.

The process will result in a web of streamers representing the interconnectedness of all the students.

Chapter Seven　　　*Suggested Student Readings*

BAYLOR, BYRD AND PETER PARNALL. *The Other Way to Listen.* New York: Charles Scribner's Sons, 1978.

BEIM AND BEIM. *Two Is a Team.* New York: Harcourt Brace, 1945.

CECIL, LAURA. *Listen to This.* New York: Greenwillow, 1987.

DURRELL, ANNE AND MARILYN SACHS, Eds. *The Big Book for Peace.* New York: Dutton, 1990.

HAZEN, NIKKI. *Grown-Ups Cry Too.* Carrboro, NC: Lollipop Power, 1973.

MANDELBAUM, PHIL. *You Be Me / I'll Be You.* California: Kane/Miller, 1990.

PAUL, PAULA. *You Can Hear a Magpie Smile.* New York: Nelson, 1980.

RINGGOLD, FAITH. *Aunt Harriet's Underground Railroad in the Sky.* New York: Crown, 1992.

SHAH, INDRIES. *World Tales.* New York: Harcourt Brace Jovanovich, 1979.

CHAPTER EIGHT

Contribution

Celebrating Service

*A*ny of us can dream, but seeking vision is always done not only to heal and fulfill one's own potential, but also to learn to use that potential to serve all our relations: the two–leggeds, the four–legged, the wingeds, those that crawl upon the Earth, and the Mother Earth herself.

—Brooke Medicine Eagle

Introduction

One of my most memorable experiences as an educational consultant was the opportunity to conduct a leadership workshop for high-school aged students from Russia.

Having grown up during the Cold War, living through the Cuban Missile Crisis with images of Kruschev pounding his shoe on the table while threatening to bury us, and going through bomb shelter drills in school as regularly as we did fire drills, did much to shape my image of the Soviet Union as the Evil Empire.

Much to my surprise and delight, I learned by using some of the activities in this book that Russian teenagers want essentially what all of us want —

to be safe and secure, to feel included and accepted, to be free to pursue their dreams, and to be able to contribute to others.

At the end of the workshop I conducted with them, these students were given $50 to spend any way they wanted. Needless to say, they were overwhelmed by the massive amounts of merchandise available in the department stores of downtown San Francisco. We had fun guessing what purchases would be made during their shopping spree. I was betting on a pair of Levis being at the top of everyone's list.

As it turned out, virtually every student decided not to spend the money, but rather to bring it home to their families to be spent on more essential items. While I was comforted to know that their values and mine have much in common, I was embarrassed to realize that they were more disciplined and less self-centered than I might have been under similar circumstances.

This final chapter extends the theme of Social Responsibility to a full global perspective. The activities encourage students to realize that their ultimate fulfillment will be found in service. Community-based and environmentally-conscious projects are suggested. The book ends on the theme of making the world a more peaceful and harmonious place for all.

My dream has always been that schools would do more than merely reflect society as it is, but that they would become learning laboratories where we adults could work together with the next generation of world citizens to discover ways of transforming society so that it is more consistent with how we would want it to be.

It is my hope that this book will be a step in that direction.

All things are connected like the blood that unites us. We did not weave the web of life, we are merely a strand in it. Whatever we do to the web, we do to ourselves.

—Chief Seattle

71

Nobel Prize Winners

> **W**inning the Prize [1963 Nobel Prize in physics] wasn't half as exciting as doing the work itself.
>
> — Maria Gaeppert Mayer

Purpose

The purpose of this activity is to inspire children to dream of making a significant contribution to humanity.

The Nobel Prize, named after the Swedish industrialist Alfred Nobel who endowed the prize, is awarded for significant contributions in the areas of literature, economics, physics, chemistry, medicine and for efforts on behalf of world peace.

The Nobel Peace Prize has been awarded to men and women from various countries over the years. Among these are:

1992   Rigoberta Menchu
Guatemalan Indian rights activist

1989   The Dalai Lama
Exiled religious and political leader of Tibet

1984   Desmond Tutu
South African Anglican Bishop and anti-apartheid activist

1979   Mother Teresa
Missionary working with the sick and destitute of Calcutta

Procedure

1.   Discuss the Nobel Peace Prize with your class.

Share the contributions of past winners. If possible use photos or film clips to enliven the presentation.

2.   Have students do a report—written and/or oral—on a Nobel Prize winner of their choice. You may have them do individual projects or work in small teams on a cooperative learning project.

Encourage students to be creative. Besides a standard report, suggest that they do a skit or play or use an interview format.

3.   Provide time for students to present their reports.

4.   Next have students think about the contributions they would like to make.

> *Imagine winning the Nobel Peace Prize 20 or 30 years from now. What would it be for? What would it say? For example, when the prize was awarded in 1992 the Nobel Committee said this about its recipient:*
>
> > *"Rigoberta Menchu stands out as a vivid symbol of peace and reconciliation across ethnic cultural and social dividing lines, in her own country, on the American Continent and in the world."*

5.   Have the students work with a partner to develop their vision and wording for the award.

6.   Have each student present the award to his or her partner in front of the whole class.

72

Lend A Hand

> *The two kinds of people on earth that I mean*
> *Are the people who lift and the people who lean.*
>
> — Ella Wheeler Wilcox

Purpose

The activity* is meant to create a visual display of the power and beauty that comes from everyone lending a helping hand. It can also be used to promote good deeds at school, at home and in the community.

Materials

A piece of white art paper (8" square is a good size) for each student, pencils and other art supplies such as crayons, colored markers, stickers, magazines, glue and scissors, and so forth

Procedure

1.   Distribute paper and art supplies and ask students to trace an outline of their hand on the paper. Students can work in groups to help each other and share materials.

2.   Next, invite students to decorate their hand drawing however they would like. For example:
      • color it one color or many colors
      • draw a tattoo
      • draw jewelry

---

* This activity was suggested by a community-service project held in San Francisco in December of 1992 as a benefit for Project Open Hand, an organization that serves free meals to people with AIDS.

- write or print their name on it as many times as will fit
- write the names of the people who help them the most or that they would most like to help.

3.   Now, have the students commit to lending a helping hand at school and home or in their community. After they have helped someone out, they can share how they lent a hand and at that point they can post their hand drawing on the wall.

Students should hold onto their drawings until such time as they were helpful to someone—this being the price of admission in the "High Five Wall."

4.   Create a "High Five Wall" by posting all the separate pages together to make one large mural.

73

Community-Service Projects

> *The contents of his [Sitting Bull's] pockets were often emptied into the hands of small, ragged little boys, nor could he understand how so much wealth should go brushing by, unmindful of the poor.*
>
> — Annie Oakley

Purpose

This activity helps students to become actively involved in contributing to their community.

Procedure

1.   Brainstorm with your students about possible community-service projects that your class or school might implement, such as:

   • a school-wide canned food drive
   • an Adopt-a-Grandparent program at a local convalescent home
   • a school-wide drive to collect toys for the local needy families in conjunction with other city groups
   • a car wash to raise funds for a local homeless shelter.
   • a planned participation in National Youth Service Day*

2.   Help the group select one that they could realistically accomplish.

---

* National Youth Service Day is organized by Youth Service America, an award-winning clearinghouse for volunteer opportunities. You can contact them to find organizations in your area that are looking for help by writing Youth Service America, Dept. P. Suite 200; 1101 15th St. N.W.; Washington, D.C. 20005-5002 or visit their Web site, www.SERVEnet.org.

3. Consider whether academic credit for student involvement seems appropriate. If so, you might discuss with them what projects might provide the greatest opportunity to learn academic skills such as math (a fundraising event), English (a letter-writing campaign), history (a multicultural experience), physical sciences (an environmentally related project), social sciences (working with senior citizens, the underprivileged), and so on.

    Establish a way of documenting the learning—perhaps an independent study contract—in order to award credit for work done on the project.

4. Once the community–service project has been selected, work with the students to identify the **purpose** of the project, the group's **goals** for the project and the specific **actions** that will need to be taken to accomplish the project.

    For example:

    -   The **purpose** of a canned food drive is to provide healthy food to people who might otherwise go hungry.

    -   Our **goal** is to collect a total of 30 cans by the end of next week.

    -   Some of the **actions** that we need to take are:
        —   Brainstorm types of canned foods that are healthy and most useful. (A good opportunity to learn about nutrition).
        —   Identify possible agencies to whom we could donate the cans.
        —   Have each one of us be responsible for one can, either bringing it in ourselves or getting someone else to donate it such as another teacher, a local merchant and so forth.
        —   Find a place to store the cans until they are all received.
        —   Find a way to deliver the cans to the agency we picked.

5. After the project is completed, hold a class meeting to discuss how it went.

    Possible discussion questions:

    "Did we accomplish our purpose?"
    "Did we achieve our goal?"
    "Was it easy or hard to do?"
    "Did anything unexpected happen?"

"Was there anything that got in our way?"
"What did we learn from doing this?"
"How do you feel about what we did?"

If you are trying to transform a brutalized society into one where people can live in dignity and hope, you begin with the empowering of the most powerless. You build from the ground up.

— Adrian Rich

74

Saving The Planet·

> *I had assumed that the Earth, the spirit of the Earth, noticed exceptions —those who wantonly damage it and those who do not. But the Earth is wise. It has given itself into the keeping of all, and all are therefore accountable.*
>
> —Alice Walker

> *The maltreatment of the natural world and its impoverishment leads to the impoverishment of the human soul. It is related to the outburst of violence in human society. To save the natural world today means to save what is human in humanity.*
>
> — Raisa M. Gorbachev

Purpose

Ecology is one area that involves all people of all cultures. Whether we are discussing the rain forests or recycling, oil spills or the ozone layer, environmental issues do not end neatly at the border of a particular country. We are indeed part of a global village.

The purpose of this activity is to instill in our children an awareness of their responsibility for the environment by starting a recycling program at their own school.

** The authors wish to acknowledge *50 Simple Things Kids Can Do To Save The Earth* by Earth Works (Kansas City: Andrews and McNeal, 1990) for giving form to this idea and for a great book of 49 other ideas.

Procedure

1. Start with a discussion about the importance of recycling focusing on the amount of paper, aluminum and glass used at school.

2. Have students spend a day noticing and recording all the places in school where paper, aluminum and glass are used such as classrooms, cafeteria, offices, labs and so forth.

3. Next discuss what would be involved in setting up a recycling center. Consider things such as:

    - a place to put containers to hold recycling materials
    - containers—large, sturdy cardboard boxes or bins—to collect paper, metal and glass.
    - signs to label containers.
    - transportation to a recycling center or out on the sidewalk if curbside pick-up is available in your area.

4. Once the recycling center is set up, how will everyone know about it and be encouraged to use it? Brainstorm with your students how to get the whole school involved. Perhaps:

    - posters
    - in-school announcements
    - contests
    - article in school newspaper
    - press releases to local newspaper, radio and TV stations.

75

World Travelers

> *Certainly, travel is more than the seeing of sights; it is a change that goes on, deep and permanent, in the ideas of living.*
>
> —Miriam Beard

Purpose

Through this activity, students get to imagine traveling around the world—visiting places they have always wanted to see, returning to their ancestral homeland or exploring an exotic locale with a totally different culture.

Their appreciation for people and customs of different cultures will be enhanced.

Procedure

1. Engage the students in a discussion of various countries and cultures around the world. Find out what places your students have already visited. Have them consider what part of the world they would like to see and what they have heard about these places. Using a large map to help students locate the various destinations would help expand their sights.

2. Have students work together in their teams or cooperative learning group to plan an itinerary of places their groups wants to visit on their world tour.

3. Establish learning centers at various places around the room and ask each team to be responsible for setting up a display of materials related to one of the cities or countries that they are planning to visit. Coordinate the process so that each team is researching a

different location. Suggest to the students that they go to a travel agency to get posters and brochures on their destination. Have them use their geography books, encyclopedia or other books from the library to learn about this country, its people, language, culture, customs, money system and so forth.

Brainstorm with your students other things they could include in their display such as:

- articles of clothing
- stamps
- magazines, newspapers
- photographs
- food
- arts and crafts.

4.   When the projects are completed, allow class time for the student teams to report on their trip, highlighting the destination on display. Let the students roam around to each of the learning centers.

5.   This could be developed into an entire unit with academic credit being given for the subject areas that the students learned about through their involvement in the project.

76

Pen Pals

> **W***hy is it that you can sometimes feel the reality of people more keenly through a letter than face to face?*
>
> —Anne Morrow Lindbergh

Purpose

For students to realize that in countries around the world there are children just like themselves with similar feelings, wants and needs.

This will help to humanize the "foreigners" and build more respect for people from different cultures.

Procedure

1. One good way of introducing this activity is to read the book *A Country Far Away* by Nigel Gray and Philippe Dupasqui (New York: Orchard Books, 1991).

    It is a delightful story of two young boys—one African and one American—with one text and two sets of illustrations showing the same actions in two very different cultures. The book ends with each child imagining that he will visit the other's country and make a friend.

2. Ask the students to think about a country that they would like to visit and perhaps make a friend.

    Since they are going to communicate in writing, they should consider possible difficulties with language and ways with which they will deal with this. Limiting the activity to countries that speak the same language as the student or finding a source for translators are two possibilities.

3. Next, the students will need to find a way to connect with children in the desired countries. One possibility is to call or write to an organization that works in this area such as:

> World Pen Pals
> 1690 Como Ave.
> St. Paul, MN 55108
> (612) 647-0191

World Pen Pals lists more than 40,000 names of people worldwide who are looking for pen pals.

Two other organizations that will line up pen pals are:

> Worldwide Friendship International
> 3749 Brice Run Rd., Suite A
> Randalls town, MD 21133

> For Our Children's Sake
> 475 Riverside Dr., Suite 828
> New York, NY 10115
> (Send self-addressed stamped envelope)

4. Have students write their letter to their pen pal and share it in teams before sending it. Team members could offer feedback and suggestions, and you could help with spelling and so forth as needed.

5. As the letters from the Pen Pals in various parts of the world begin to be received by the students, allow them to share these and post them for others to read.

7 7

A World of Friends·

> **T**o *him in whom love dwells,*
> *the whole world is but one family.*
>
> — Buddha

Purpose

The local chapter of the American Red Cross will provide you with twenty-five empty boxes which when filled, they will send to a country you choose. For information write:

American Red Cross, National Headquarters
International/Youth Services
Attn. - Friendship Boxes
Washington, DC 20006

This is a fun way for your students to connect with children in other parts of the world. You may want to start with needy children in your own neighborhood, city, state or other parts of the United States.

Procedure

1.   Discuss with your students the idea of sending boxes of gifts to needy children throughout the world. Consider:

   Is this something you would like to do?

   What kinds of things would we send?

· This activity was suggested by an excellent book of projects for "kids who want to help people, animals and the world we live in." *The Helping Hands Handbook* by Patricia Adams and Jean Marzollo (Random House: New York, 1992).

What kinds of things would you like to receive if it were being sent to you?

What countries would we consider sending gifts?

What do we know about conditions in these countries?

If you were a child in this country would you like to get from children in America?

As the discussion proceeds, develop a list of items that might be put in these boxes such as soap, combs, marbles, photographs, arts and crafts, and so forth.

2. You may want to contact the Red Cross yourself to get all the necessary information and request the boxes or you may want to include students in this process. Students could brainstorm the questions that they have and help draft the letter.

3. With your students, decide if each student will fill a box or if they will work in teams.

4. Provide a place in the classroom for the items that are collected to be stored until the boxes are filled and sent.

5. Class time could be used to make items such as book markers, greeting cards and so forth.

78

World Leaders

> **W**hy do we need leaders in a free country? I would answer that the leader's function is to determine, in any crisis, which of our possible selves will act.
>
> — Lyman Bryson

Purpose

As the next generation of world citizens, our children have a stake in the future and how today's leaders are impacting that future.

This activity helps students create a vision of the world in which they want to live and how they might be able to influence that future.

Procedure

1.   Brainstorm with your students all the world leaders they are able to name. They may need to do some research to add names to those that they know.

2.   Ask the students to imagine that these world leaders will be gathered for a conference on the future and that the students will have a chance to present to these leaders. The topic of the presentation is "The world we want and what we need to do about it now."

3.   Hand out the worksheet, The World We Want and invite the students to use this as a way of structuring their thoughts.

4.   Let the students work in teams or in a cooperative learning group to prepare and practice their presentations.

5.   Schedule a "Future of the World Conference" at which students will present their vision and suggestions. You may want to invite

some guests to serve as the panel of world leaders. These guests could include other teachers or administrators, parents, local business people or community leaders, or older students.

6.   Have each team of students do their presentations.

7.   Afterwards bring the students together into a class circle and discuss how the conference went.

Possible discussion questions:

How do you feel about the conference?

What did you like about the presentations?

Were there common themes from the different presentations?

Did you say what you wanted to the world leaders?

Is there anything you would do differently if you really had the opportunity to be present at such a conference?

The World We Want Worksheet

1.   My **vision** of a better world is:

    _____
    _____
    _____
    _____

2.   A better world would have **more**:

    _____
    _____
    _____

3.   A better world would have **less**:

    _____
    _____
    _____
    _____

4.   In a better world **all people** would:

    _____
    _____
    _____
    _____

5.   If I were a **world leader** I would:

    _____
    _____
    _____

6.   **All of us** must work together to:

    _____
    _____
    _____
    _____

79

World Leaders:

The Televised Summit

> *What the best and wisest parent wants for his own child, that must be what the community wants for all its children.*
>
> —John Dewey

Purpose

This final video recording activity will give your students an opportunity to internalize the lessons learned about social responsibility.

Materials

Video camera or camcorder, VCR playback equipment, TV monitor and blank video tape.

Procedure

Structured Approach

Use the previous activity, World Leaders and record it as if it were a satellite program being simultaneously broadcast around the world.

Creative Approach

Use the worksheet Part IV—Key Learnings to select a topic, decide on format for the TV show and let students run with it.

8 0

I'd Like to Teach the World to Sing

> **W**hat good is music? None ... and that is the point. To the world and its states and armies and factories and Leaders, music says, 'You are irrelevant'; and arrogant and gentle as a god, to the suffering man it says only 'Listen'. For being saved is not the point. Music saves nothing. Merciful, uncaring, it denies and breaks down all the shelters, the houses men build for themselves, that they may see the sky.
>
> — Ursula K. Le Guin

> **W**hile I listened, music was to my soul what the atmosphere is to my body; it was the breath of my inward life. I felt, more deeply than ever, that music is the highest symbol of the infinite and holy.
>
> — Lydia Maria Child

Purpose

For many of us, music has a healing affect. Music can transcend time and place, and unite people in "perfect harmony."

This activity is meant to be an uplifting celebration of humanity in all its wonderful diversity.

Procedure

1. With your students select a song such as, "I'd Like To Teach The World To Sing In Perfect Harmony," that is uplifting and has an easy melody.

2. Get help from students, parents, other teachers and community members to translate the lyrics of this song in all the languages spoken by your students so that all cultures are included. You may also want to include any additional languages that are important to your students.

3. Teach yourself how to sing the song in each of the different languages.

4. Plan a time when you can have a fiesta—a day to *celebrate diversity*. Brainstorm with your students whom they would like to invite:

   - just their class
   - one or a few other classes
   - the entire school
   - other schools
   - their families
   - other community members.

   Decide what kinds of activities they would like to plan for the day:

   - multicultural food fair
   - art and crafts
   - dance and music
   - showing their TV programs
   - doing other activities from the book, and of course,
   - a sing-a-long — in the many languages of our cultures — "in perfect harmony."

Part IV—Key Learnings

o—⊾ I listen carefully to hear what the other person means.

o—⊾ I look for peaceful solutions to conflict.

o—⊾ I allow others to have their own point of view even if it is different from mine.

o—⊾ I know that I can and do make a difference.

o—⊾ I am able to work as part of a team.

o—⊾ I feel good about myself when I am serving others who are less fortunate.

o—⊾ I choose my friends wisely.

o—⊾ I am responsible for taking good care of the planet.

o—⊾ I know when to say no.

o—⊾ I envision a better world where people take care of each other.

o—⊾ I am able to solve problems.

Part IV—Teacher Checklist
Turning Problems into Opportunities for Learning

❑   Have I come to appreciate that I am probably not going to change the world overnight, and that building respect for oneself and others is on-going process?

❑   Am I observing what's working as well as what's not working in a nonjudgmental way so that I can learn from the experience and constantly improve?

❑   Have I been encouraging my students to be open-minded and accepting of "failures" as steps on the road to success?

❑   When incidents of stereotyping, prejudice and discrimination occur, have I developed the skills to turn these into learning opportunities for the students involved?

❑   Am I able to stay calm and objective rather than react in an emotional way so that I can maintain the role of coach in helping students deal with these situations?

❑   Have I learned how to coach students who have been on the receiving end of ethnic slurs or other types of put-downs in a way that empowers them rather than promotes feelings of either victimization or revenge?

❑   Have I learned how to coach students who were the perpetrators of ethnic slurs or other types of put-downs so that they develop greater sensitivity, increase their awareness and act differently in the future?

❑   Do we hold regular class meetings so that students can discuss their feelings and solve their own problems?

❑   Am I working with community resources to help create healthy and productive activities to keep my students involved in life-enhancing experiences?

Chapter Eight   *Suggested Student Readings*

ADAMS, PATRICIA AND JEAN MARZOLLO. *The Helping Hands Handbook.* New York: Random House, 1992.

COER, ELEANOR B. *Sadako and the Thousand Paper Cranes.* New York: Macmillan, Inc., 1979.

EARTHWORKS GROUP. *50 Simple Things Kids Can Do to Save the Earth.* Kansas City: Andrews and McMeel, 1990.

GRAY, NIGET AND PHILIPPE DUPASQUIES. *A Country Far Away.* New York: Orchard Books, 1988.

JEFFERS, SUSAN. *Brother Eagle, Sister Sky: A Message from Chief Seattle.* New York: Dial, 1991.

PERETZ, I.C. *The Case Against the Wind and Other Stories,* trans and adapted by Esther Hautzig. New York: Macmillan, 1975.

REFERENCES

BANKS, JAMES A. *Teaching Strategies for Ethnic Studies (5th ed.)* Needham Heights, MA: Allyn and Bacon, 1991.

— *Multiethnic Education: Theory and Practice (2nd ed.).* Needham Heights, MA: Allyn and Bacon, 1988.

BANKS, JAMES A. AND CHERRY A. MCGEE BANKS (eds). *Multicultural Education: Issues and Perspectives.* Needham Heights, MA: Allyn and Bacon, 1989.

BOARD OF EDUCATION OF THE CITY OF NEW YORK. *Children of the Rainbow.* New York: Department of Education, 1991.

BRANDEN, NATHANIEL. *The Power of Self-Esteem.* Deerfield Beach, FL: Health Communications, Inc., 1992.

CANFIELD, JACK AND FRANK SICCONE. *101 Ways To Develop Students Self - Esteem and Responsibility* Needham Heights, MA: Allyn and Bacon, 1995.

CLEVELAND PUBLIC SCHOOLS. *Pupil Adjustment in a Desegrated Setting.* Cleveland: Cleveland Public Schools, 1978.

COMMUNITY BOARD PROGRAMS. Training High School Conflict Managers. San Francisco, CA: 1986.

DUNHAM, CARROL et al. *Mamatoto: A Celebration of Birth.* New York: Penguin Books, 1991.

CUMMINS, JIM. *Empowering Minority Students.* Sacramento, CA: California Association for Bilingual Education, 1989.

FRANCIS, DAVE AND DON YOUNG. *Improving Work Groups: A Practical Manual for Team Building,* San Diego: University Associates, 1972.

LAZEAR, DAVID. *Seven Ways of Teaching.* Palatine, IL: Skylight Publishing, 1991.

NIETO, SONIA. *Affirming Diversity: The Sociopolitical Context of Multicultural Education.* New York: Longman, 1992.

PFIEFFER J. WILLIAM AND JOHN E. JONES, eds., *The 1972 Annual Handbook for Group Facilitators.* San Diego, University Associates, 1972.

SHAFTEL, FANNIE R. AND GEORGE SHAFTEL. *Role-Playing in the Curriculum (2nd ed.).* Engelwood Cliffs, NJ: Prentice Hall, 1982.

TIEDT, PAMELA L. AND IRIS M. TIEDT. *Multicultural Teaching* (Third Edition). Needham Heights, MA: Allyn and Bacon, 1990